The Little Kingdom

The Little Kingdom

BY HUGHIE CALL

with illustrations by Gloria Kamen

HOUGHTON MIFFLIN COMPANY BOSTON

The Riverside Press Cambridge

1964

FIRST PRINTING   R

COPYRIGHT © 1964 BY HUGHIE CALL
ALL RIGHTS RESERVED INCLUDING THE RIGHT TO
REPRODUCE THIS BOOK OR PARTS THEREOF IN ANY FORM.
LIBRARY OF CONGRESS CATALOG CARD NUMBER: 64-12871
PORTIONS OF THIS BOOK HAVE PREVIOUSLY
APPEARED IN *Redbook* MAGAZINE.

The Riverside Press
CAMBRIDGE · MASSACHUSETTS
PRINTED IN THE U.S.A.

for Tom

The Little Kingdom

Chapter One

WE NAMED HER LOUISE but she was never called anything but Wezie. She was born into a man's world — on a ranch in the high sheep country of Montana. She was a bit of lagniappe given to Tom and me when our sons Andy and Leigh were school age and when we thought our family complete. It could never have been complete without Wezie. She was the leaven in the loaf, the special ingredient that seasoned everyday life on our ranch.

She came into the world the way she lived in it — tumultuously, joyously and ahead of time; so far ahead that the doctor could not be reached and she arrived on her own. There was a fearless independence about her from the start and she rushed through life like one of Montana's sparkling mountain streams.

"Aren't you ready, Mother?" she would ask, anxious to be off, anxious to fill every hour of every day with all the things she wanted to do. There were never enough hours.

She was a sturdy little towhead with a warm, impartial love for people and a passion for animals, wild or tame, on four feet or limping. Our ranch, to Wezie, was more than a business enterprise. It was a little kingdom inhabited by her family, the men who worked for us and the furred and feathered creatures which sought sanctuary within the four-strand barbed wire fence that enclosed our land.

Over the years Wezie had some strange pets. They march through my memory in a pathetic and sometimes comical procession. There was Lady, a lame deer; Missie, an orphan antelope fawn; Sweet Adeline, a wild Canada goose; Madame Cluck, a ruffed grouse, and Bitsie, a "bum" (motherless) lamb. There were crows, pheasants, axolotl (walking fish), snakes and dogs. Dogs *ad infinitum*.

Of course there were the horses but they didn't come under this category. Horses were on the same plane as the family where Wezie was concerned. They were kinfolk, as important as the rest of us. She talked to them as she did to anybody else; and every piece of horseflesh on the place — tame or wild or just plain mean — understood her language, too.

This was no wonder. From the time she could walk, a horse's back was as familiar as a chair. First she rode with her father on Dolly, his big bay mare. Perched between Tom and the saddle horn, she travelled up hill and down valley the length and breadth of our ranch.

She visited sheep camps and learned, first hand, the vagaries of sheep and the unpredictable whims of their herders. She knew what a "section corner" was before she knew her alphabet, and could spot an over-grazed range before she could read. She was interested in every small thing that concerned the sheep or the range — far more so than either of her brothers.

I remember scolding Leigh because he rebelled when told he'd have to help drive a band of old ewes to the railroad on a Labor Day weekend. "Wezie's begging to go," I said. "If you boys were half as interested in the operation of this ranch we'd be rich."

"I was interested too when I was little and rode places with Dad," Leigh told me. "Wezie's got it easy. She don't have to haul old ewes off their backs when they get down, or coax 'em across bridges when they balk."

Andy looked up from a trap he was mending and grinned. "Wezie don't have to skin 'em either, when they give up the ghost."

"She'd be willing to," Tom said slowly, guessing even then that neither of our sons would ever want to be ranchers, would ever be interested in carrying on a business that he'd spent a lifetime wresting from blizzards and droughts, hail and floods.

And there was Wezie, always willing and eager, always pleading to go. This soon became a problem. "I have to sneak through the back corral if I get away without her." Tom looked harassed and I wondered then as I was to wonder many times in the future how one small girl could so temper the life of a big, decisive man like Tom.

"You could do one of two things," I reminded. "You could say *no*, or you could buy her a horse of her own."

This was a subject we'd argued for the past two years and oddly enough it was I who wanted Wezie to have a horse. She was six now. Andy and Leigh had ridden alone at five. But Tom was afraid for Wezie. "She's too reckless," he said. "She's not afraid of man or devil."

"It would have to be just the right horse," I insisted, "but you could find one if you'd try."

He found the horse early that summer, a pinto gelding, part Welch, part Shetland, but mostly heart. The pony belonged to a rancher who lived near the Point of Rocks, not far from Dillon. His two sons had outgrown the little horse and were anxious to find just the right home for him. That particular week we were hauling wool to a Dillon warehouse and Tom told Shorty, the truck driver, he could load the pony on his way home.

Wezie wanted to go too; but it was a long, rough trip. Tom said *No* and stayed with it. She finally accepted defeat; but was restless all that day, awaiting Shorty's return. We were helping the cook shell green peas on the back porch when we heard the truck rattle across a cattle guard.

Wezie scrambled to her feet, upsetting a pan of peas which skittered in all directions. "That's Shorty, Mother! Hurry! Hurry!" She caught my hand and we raced through the gate, across the creek bridge, to the barnyard. Another four-legged member of our family was arriving and not in a casual manner like the rest of the horses had.

The minute the ramp was adjusted and the end gate raised the little horse shot out like an arrow from a taut bowstring. We were soon to learn that the pony never walked. He galloped, loped or ran; and he would have lit out that very day if Shorty hadn't grabbed his halter and yanked him to a standstill.

"Name's Patches," Shorty told us. "Anyway that's what

those boys called him." Patches reared and was jerked back on all fours. "If he was mine I'd call him Beelzebub. He's a mean little booger. Took three of us to load him."

"He's not mean!" Wezie made a flying leap and flung both arms as far as they would reach about the gelding's neck. "He's a beautiful horse." She pressed her cheek against the rough brown mane.

Patches laid back his ears, snorted and stepped sideways. Obviously he was unaccustomed to such extravagant affection and not ready to give his friendship so lightly. He might be small but he had a mind of his own. What he lacked in size he more than made up for in speed and spirit. In the weeks that followed we discovered that there were few horses on the place which could outrun him and then only after he had half killed himself trying to keep in the lead. In his own mind, he was as big as the rest of the horses and every time Wezie led him out of the corral, he put on a show to prove it — rearing, walling his eyes, snorting and pawing the earth like a pint size Bucephalus.

But the minute she put foot in the stirrup, an astounding change came over him. The little horse quieted immediately, as if he knew he'd been entrusted with a precious burden. And as long as that burden was Wezie he behaved, but he never let another girl child ride him.

Patches' former owner had assured us that the pony was well trained and had no bad habits other than being a little choosy about his riders. The rancher neglected to mention that Patches was as curious as a magpie, for instance, and as meddlesome as a monkey. Anything he didn't understand he investigated with the fervor of a sheep dog at a gopher hole. A closed paper carton, a tied-up sack, gloves laid on a fence post and forgotten, sheep pelts stretched on a corral panel — nothing escaped his attention.

He had to be shut out of the yard (the day after his arrival) because he spied a flapping sheet and worried it back and forth until the clothesline broke. Chased through the gate by an irate cook, he nosed around the chicken house, sent a setting hen squawking off the nest, sampled the straw she'd been sitting on, and cracked a dozen guinea eggs that Jack, our Irish choreboy, had paid a fancy price for.

Jack heard the squawking biddy and bolted out of the bunkhouse, blood in his eye. Jack was sixty, with a thatch of snow-white hair and the finely chiselled features of a medieval saint. But there was nothing saintly about Jack. The old fellow was as tough as a frostbitten gourd and as blasphemous as a sailor's parrot.

He'd served a hitch in the English navy but not by choice. "They gi' me the Queen's shilling," he'd weep when he'd had a few drinks and only Wezie would sympathize. The rest of us had heard this story many times and always when Jack was working up to his annual spree which would last until his money was gone and his credit exhausted.

Wezie and I heard the squawking old biddy too, and rushed outdoors but Jack reached the chicken yard first. He was chunking Patches with everything he could lay a hand to. A mop handle sailed through the air, a rock which just missed the pony's impudent departing hooves. A bigger rock . . .

"Don't you dare chunk my horse!" Wezie watched Patches disappear in the canyon underbrush and turned on Jack, her eyes blazing.

"Stop it! You stop it!" She caught his arm, tried to take the rock. "You've hurt Patches' feelings."

"Feelings?" Jack bellowed. "That limb of Satan ain't got feelings. Just you come and look at what he done." He hauled Wezie inside the chicken house and showed her the broken guinea eggs.

"But you shouldn't have left the door open. He didn't know. Maybe he was hungry." She burst into tears. "Maybe he won't come back."

Now Jack could have watched some adult put through a meat grinder if he deserved it and never have batted an eye but Wezie's tears unnerved him. From the day she was born he had loved and watched over her, fought her battles, mended her toys and doctored her ailing pets.

"Quit your crying." He tossed the rock over his shoulder. "We're going to find that little divil and when we do we'll teach him some manners." His voice was gruff but a big hand reached for Wezie's and they set off up Wigwam Canyon together. They were back in ten minutes and Wezie was riding Patches. Jack, a deflated Irishman, was trotting alongside, his fingers laced in the pony's mane.

"Jack and Patches are going to be friends after all," Wezie told me when I tucked her in that night. "And Mother — Patches is beginning to like me too. I can tell."

Before the month was up Patches adored her. His devotion was as touching as it was ridiculous. He'd wait outside the gate for her every morning, pacing the fence, snorting and whinnying at Coalie and Midge, retired sheep dogs which had the run of the yard. The fat old dogs would waddle out growling but soon the weight of their years would catch up with them and they'd waddle back to doze on the vine-covered porch. Patches quieted then but the instant one of the dogs showed up in the yard he'd whinny and snort. These tantrums were a source of amusement to everyone on the ranch except Wezie. She worried lest Patches catch his hoof in the woven wire fence, or get cut on the barbed wire strand that was stretched along the top.

"I wish he wouldn't, Mother."

"Never mind, honey. The little fellow's just showing off. He'll calm down after he's lived here awhile."

"No, Mother. He won't as long as Coalie and Midge stay in the yard and he can't. He's afraid I'll like them best," she told me with an understanding far beyond her years.

And so went the summer — the kind of summer that sheep people dream about and seldom see. Heartwarming sun for days on end and then, just at the right time gentle rains that soaked into the earth and nurtured grass so tall you couldn't see the sheep when they bedded down in it. Hay men stayed on the job that summer and even whistled and sang at their work. There was a cook in the kitchen. And Wezie, threading in and out of the ranch activities, through shearing, through haying, through shipping the lambs. Always on Patches. You seldom saw one without the other.

There's no way of explaining the tie that existed between

the little girl and the little horse. Perhaps it was their lively curiosity — the explorations and discoveries they shared when they rode. Perhaps that trait of complete and utter fearlessness both of them had.

Even the first summer, when Wezie was so small she had to crawl up on the manger to put the bit in Patches' mouth, there was an indefinable something between them that was barely short of fey.

She didn't have to teach Patches; Patches knew what she wanted before he was told. Long before we thought Wezie old enough, the two of them were jumping ditches and fences. They were taking chances that would have curled our hair had we known.

One morning when Tom was haying he got a scare that sent him leaping for his own horse. Looking toward the foothills he'd seen Wezie try a pole fence on Patches and get a nasty spill. He was a quarter mile away and had visions of the pony kicking or dragging her before he could come to the rescue. When he arrived, Wezie was sitting on the ground picking leaves and dirt out of her hair and talking to Patches who grazed nearby.

"You might have been killed," I scolded later, "that horse might have kicked you."

"Patches wouldn't hurt me." She was a little indignant. "I've got spilled before. Patches just stands still until I get out of the way. Patches always knows where I am, Mother."

I found that the little horse was indeed to be trusted; that he seemed to know exactly where Wezie was every moment, topside or not. One day from an upstairs window

I saw her try to jump a narrow place on Wigwam Creek. Patches stumbled and she sailed right over his head. Before I could move, the pony reared so close to her body that my heart stood still. But he twisted clear, brought his hooves down at a safe distance and stood statue-still until she got to her feet. I heaved a sigh of relief and went back to my work. From that day on I worried no more.

Chapter Two

Wigwam canyon stretches from sun to sun and was so called by old-timers after a narrow, willow-lined stream that courses through its length. The creek got its name from Indians who once hunted over this section of Montana and whose tepee stones can still be seen on a flat above the house. For years we never plowed new ground without turning up hundreds of arrowheads.

Toward the west, looking down the canyon from the wide clearing where the home ranchhouse is located, the cliffs fall away and ease gently into the valley of the Madison River. The house, a foursquare, completely masculine place of abode stands out in grim relief against the canyon walls.

Tom had picked the site carefully with shelter from the bitter winds in mind. But the house was a more casual matter. He described it in a letter before we were married: *Eight rooms, porch around the front and west side.* Then he threw in this bit. *I drew the plans myself, one night after supper.*

I could well believe this when I got my first glimpse of

the place. It was an exact, stark replica of the houses I'd drawn in kindergarten down to a curl of smoke that spiralled from the chimney. Inside, the rooms were devoid of anything as frivolous as curtains at the windows or rugs on the scrubbed pine floors. It was furnished after a fashion — from a mail order catalogue, I later learned.

Accustomed to a certain easy grace of living in my native Texas I wondered if I could ever get used to its austerity. It took time — a lot of time. But the canyon I loved at once, especially that part upcreek from the house.

The canyon was a place of mystery and enchantment. Sometimes it narrowed until there was scarcely room to edge between its towering walls and a tangle of willows and wild berry bushes that hugged the banks of the little stream on either side. Then there'd be patches of ground that widened into fairy-like meadows carpeted throughout spring and summer with forget-me-nots, white and pale lavender violets, birds-bills and bluebells.

Mushrooms grew in the little meadows too, springing up overnight after a rain. Watercress was plentiful, all along the creek, emerald green in the dappled sunlight of summer; frosty green with a sparkling snow fringe in winter. *Weeds* the ranchmen called it, and I shall never forget the horror on their faces the first and only time I served them watercress salad.

Actually, I did not fully explore the canyon, except that part within hailing distance of the house, until the children were old enough to make discoveries of their own. The canyon drew all three, but for Wezie it had a pull that was almost a physical thing. To her the canyon was a place of ever-changing interest and delight.

There was scarcely a day in summer that she did not ride in and out of the willows on the creek searching for arrowheads, wild flowers, fossils or turkey nests. Frequently, on Patches' back, she climbed to a ledge of rock half way up the canyon. From this height she could look down at the beaver dams and watch the matriarch Sassy dive and cavort with her kittens. Sassy was "down there" and Wezie was "up here." Geographically they never got any closer. Nevertheless, Wezie thought of Sassy as a friend. She was enormously interested in each new family of kittens, but sometimes critical of their mother's discipline.

"I think Sassy's too strict with her children," she told me. "One of the little fellows wouldn't go down the slide this afternoon. He was afraid, Mother, but Sassy made him go. She hauled off and gave him an awful wallop with her tail."

"Young beavers have to be taught to handle themselves in water, Wezie."

"But the little thing was *afraid*, Mother. And Sassy didn't have to be so rough."

"The kittens have to know how to slide into the water quickly in case of danger. Don't worry, Sassy's a good mother."

A better mother than I, perhaps. Our children were as free as the Chinook winds. They journeyed when and where they wished within the boundaries of the ranch; roving the mountains on horseback, or exploring the canyon on foot. Their projects were inexhaustible and time meant nothing to them. Once they dug for days on an Indian mound only to discover that someone else had dug first and left just a few blanched bones and scraps of leather. But this project was high adventure while it lasted.

The boys, nosing around in the willows, another summer, ran on to the abandoned shaft of an old gold mine. Some of its timbers had collapsed but they crawled in and out of the rubble, making big plans to put the mine on a paying basis. When they burst into the tool shed for a pick and shovel Tom collared them and forbade them to go near the mine again. He warned they could be pinned by collapsing timbers or even buried alive. The boys obeyed because Tom, unlike their mother, never had to forbid them twice about the same thing. But I think they always felt there was a fortune waiting just out of their reach in that mine and that some day they would find it.

In the meantime, they had to lower their sights so they turned to trapping muskrat, mink and weasel along the creek. This was a profitable business but Wezie would have no part in it. Wezie grieved over every small, still creature . . .

"Why do people have to wear fur?" she asked one day as we watched her brothers load pelts into a fur buyer's truck.

"People have to keep warm, Wezie."

"But not with *fur* — " Her voice broke and she left me abruptly.

However she did not seem to feel any qualms about very old, long-dead bones and was just as tireless and enthusiastic as the boys when they hunted fossils along the creek.

Thousands of years ago glaciers had rubbed and gouged and ground away at the old volcanic mountains that were part of the Gravelly Range which towered above the ranch. As the ice melted these glaciers gave up their treasures and deposited some on the canyon floor. The three children unearthed many fine, well-preserved fossils and eventually had a collection of which they could be proud.

Wild gooseberries, yellow currants and raspberries thrived in the canyon too and you could not walk far without hearing little whisper flurries in the underbrush for pheasant and grouse lived there. Occasionally wild geese paused on their migration flight to Canada and nested in our canyon.

It was here we found the egg that hatched Sweet Adeline and ironically it was Patches who first saw the ravaged nest and slowed his pace to investigate so that Wezie became curious too.

Patches didn't know that this innocent looking egg would one day soon bring forth a lively contender for Wezie's affections and cause him many an hour of jealousy and frustration.

Chapter Three

UNAWARE OF IMPENDING TROUBLE Patches came tit-tuping back to the house in his usual jaunty fashion — head high, mane and tail flying. Wezie slid out of the saddle and rushed indoors to tell me about the egg.

"It's just a little way up the canyon, Mother," she tugged at my hands. "Please come."

It was more than a little way but the lone egg was still warm in a litter of shell. "A wild goose egg." I picked it up. "Coyotes must have eaten the rest of the clutch."

"You shouldn't have touched it, Mother. Now the wild goose won't come back."

"Let's take the egg and put it under a setting hen." The mother goose wouldn't be coming back. I'd seen something I didn't want Wezie to see — a pile of bones and feathers half hidden by some serviceberry bushes.

She hovered close while I made a poke of my apron and rolled the egg in. "Will it really hatch?"

"Let's find out. That old biddy of Jack's is still trying to set."

We started down the canyon single file, Wezie reining Patches frequently when he swung into a gallop. At the chicken house we found Jack's old biddy still on the nest. She seemed in a trance until I slipped the egg under her. Then she raised up, regarded it excitedly and pushed it around in the straw with her beak.

"She's trying to get rid of it," Wezie cried out.

But the hen was only looking the egg over; a moment later she settled down with a contented fluff of her feathers, and closed her eyes.

"You're wasting your time," Jack grumbled when I asked him not to drive her away from the nest any more. "She's wore all the feathers off her breastbone. There ain't enough warmth in her to hatch a robin's egg."

"Let her make-believe then — have fun for a change. Think how patient she's been all this month."

Jack had long since ceased to waste time on my fancies. He grunted and stalked away.

Wezie and I went often to the chicken house to make sure the hen was still on her nest. She not only was but each day became increasingly protective of that lone egg. The moment either of us stepped through the door she let out a sound that was half way between a squawk and a cackle. The first time I tried to jack her up to take a look at the egg she pounced at my wrist and made a blood blister. Thereafter I used a stick.

We had no way of knowing how long the mother goose had been sitting on that nest up the canyon. My closest

THE LITTLE KINGDOM 21

neighbor and friend, Mrs. Bennetts, who was also my en-
cyclopedia where ranch matters were concerned, told me
the incubation period for a domestic goose egg was twenty-
eight days. She didn't know about the wild variety.

Our egg hatched in two weeks. Jack brought the news
to the house and Wezie and I followed him back to the
brooding pen. Wezie was quiet, which surprised me.
She'd been so interested, so eager for the egg to hatch.

"Aren't you glad?" I asked her as we hurried across the
bridge.

"I wonder where the real mother goose is?" Her voice
was troubled. "She laid that egg and sat on her nest for
two whole weeks and now a chicken's going to have her
baby."

But she was no longer sad when she saw the gosling
which was then several hours old. Except for a baby turkey there is no creature alive so ludicrously lovable as a
baby goose — a ball of gray and white down, balanced on
stout little legs and awkward webbed feet; a spoon-like
bill constantly in motion, and round bright eyes.

The fight was gone out of the mother hen. She was
bone weary. Her breast was completely bare of feathers
and she walked with a nautical roll. She was proud of the
gosling, if somewhat bewildered. The little thing behaved
in what must have seemed to her an extremely odd manner.
Adventurous, swashbuckling, the strange creature refused
to stay close to its mother's side like a proper chick and
from the first made independent forays into the brush along
the creek.

The hen scratched and chittered frantically, urging the

gosling to come back and see the worm she'd found for its
dinner. Apparently the gosling didn't understand chicken
language; it refused to come at her call. In the end she'd
be forced to dive into the bushes and chase it out.

The contrary little goose had another pastime that upset
its mother still more. We had a lot of rain that year and
she (we knew our gosling's gender now) loved to paddle
around in the rain. One of the funniest sights I ever saw
was the poor old biddy drenched and wing feathers dragging, but still trying her best to chase the gosling back
into the chicken house. And having no luck.

At this stage Wezie's sympathies were all with the hen.
She tried to help her by inveigling the gosling out of the
brush with tidbits from the kitchen. Soon the greedy, un-
grateful creature preferred Wezie's company to that of its
mother.

But the little goose earned her board — every crumb and
kernel of it — by the entertainment she furnished the
whole ranch that summer. She was self-assured to the
point of arrogance and had an odd habit of gabbling and
hissing as she ambled about the chicken yard.

"Like a little old lady singing to herself," I said one
morning at breakfast and it wasn't a week before the men
in the bunkhouse were calling her Sweet Adeline.

Wezie didn't like the name at first. "They're making
fun of her," she said, "and she does the very best she can."
But the name was so apt she grew accustomed to it too.

Adeline was almost as curious as Patches and this trait
frequently got her into trouble. One morning we heard a
frantic, hysterical clucking. Wezie and I rushed outdoors

and found the mother hen scurrying up and down the ditch bank. The gosling, bobbing around in the ditch like a cork, was completely beyond her control.

Adeline chose a bad day to take her first swim. Our neighbor, Mr. Thayer, had just opened the weir to let his irrigation water come through. The current was strong but there was nothing I could do about it. While this wide deep ditch crossed our home place it nevertheless belonged to Mr. Thayer on the next ranch. Our little gosling was the helpless victim of the laws of water right.

Poor Adeline was not concerned with water rights at the moment. She was terrified and paddling desperately to make the shore. But the current was too much for her. I had to hang on to Wezie to keep her from jumping in after the goose.

Tom heard the commotion and came running from the corral.

"Save Adeline, Daddy!" Wezie shrieked.

Adeline was almost out of sight now, a diminutive bark on a troublous sea.

"Where will she end up?" I asked Tom.

"In Thayer's hayfield if she doesn't get stuck in the fence between our places." He chuckled. "I've heard of 'gone goslings' all my life but this is the first time I ever saw one."

"I don't think that's funny," I said looking down at Wezie's stricken face.

Tom was instantly contrite. "I'm sorry, honey." He swung his little girl up in his arms and hugged her. "I'll get the truck. Maybe we can head Adeline off."

The three of us piled into the pick-up and drove at breakneck speed over rocks and ruts and hummocks of grass, afraid any moment would be the last for that bit of gray fluff careening along in the turbulent water. A tree branch sailed past, almost snagged her.

Wezie hid her face against Tom's sleeve. "She'll be drowned, Daddy!"

But Adeline made it safely through the woven wire fence and we caught up with her just before she was swept into one of a maze of ditches that criss-crossed Mr. Thayer's field. Adeline would really be a gone gosling if she sailed down a ditch flanked on either side by alfalfa already four inches high.

Unaware of her danger Adeline was having a lovely time in the quieter water, paddling around and around in gosling ecstasy, diving, surfacing . . . She was not a bit grateful to be rescued and struggled and hissed all the way home. The minute Wezie put her down she made a beeline for the ditch. Tom snagged her by a leg and shut her up in the brooding pen.

"You'll lose her if she runs free," he warned. "You can't keep her away from Thayer's ditch now she's tried it out."

"She's a wild goose," Wezie said slowly and Tom understood.

"Don't you worry. The mother hen will look after her and in another month she'll be big enough to look after herself."

But the mother hen succumbed soon after this, from frustration I felt sure. Adeline, with no mother to protect her from the setting hens, had to be moved to a much smaller pen. Outraged, she paced the enclosure, gabbling and hissing her indignation, poking her spoon-like bill out through the fence wire. Wezie pitied the little goose and frequently took her to the playhouse for a change of scene.

Up until this time Patches had regarded Adeline with a lofty indifference. So long as she was shut behind a woven wire fence he scarcely knew she was on the place. But he took it hard when Wezie carried the goose to her playhouse and shut the door. Since Adeline was always out of his reach and protected by Wezie he was helpless to do more than circle the playhouse, snort and paw the earth.

Eventually Tom decided it would be safe to give Adeline her freedom and on that day Patches was waiting for her. They met head-on at the water trough. The surprised Adeline was catapulted through the air, feathers flying, and Patches kept going.

Unhurt, but groggy, Adeline staggered away. Some goose sense told her that this was no accident and the next time she saw Patches she stretched her neck, hissed hideously and made for him. She wound up flattened against the chicken house. She was cannier after that encounter. Figuring that Patches had the advantage in a frontal attack, she attacked from the rear.

She'd hide in the bushes until the little horse came trotting by, then, without a sound she'd dive in, strike, and be shaking her feathers at a safe distance before Patches could whirl and lash out with his hooves.

This was a running battle that never ceased and the ignominy of it was that Adeline, equipped with wing power, always came out the victor. Wezie hated this conflict and tried to keep Patches and Adeline apart.

"Adeline will find out she's a goose afterwhile; then

she'll go about her goose business and leave Patches alone,"
I said.

But Adeline didn't go about her goose business or let
Patches alone, although she did spend more and more of
her time in the playhouse with Wezie. One day I heard
Andy's hilarious laughter and Wezie's voice screaming,
"Don't you dare make fun of my goose! You get away
from here."

I ran out to settle the argument and found Wezie kicking at her brother's shins. Adeline was clasped in her arms,
and what a goose! She was dressed in doll-size baby
clothes, complete with bootees, cap and blanket. The
sight unstrung me. When I got control of my voice I said,
"This isn't like you, Wezie. You know Adeline doesn't
like that get-up."

"She does. She loves it, Mother. And she loves to ride
in the doll buggy too. Wait and I'll show you."

She trundled her doll carriage out of the playhouse and
settled Adeline down on the pillows. The idiotic gosling
lay there in blissful content, one beady eye closed, the
other open as though she was watching our reaction. She
was clowning the part.

As the goose matured it was plain that she had been born
to "tread the boards." Her histrionic talents brought howls
of laughter from everyone on the ranch.

Wezie forgot her dolls and appropriated their costumes
to adorn Adeline. I looked out one morning to see the
gosling strutting up and down in front of the playhouse, her
white feathered rear switching importantly under the
folds of a full-skirted red organdy dress — the tips of her

wings modishly peeping out of wide, beruffled sleeves.

I laughed until the tears rolled down my cheeks. That crazy goose! She loved dressing up! Aware of an audience Sweet Adeline was stepping high, singing her gay little song.

Before that summer was over I realized that our attention had gone to Adeline's head. She was no longer content to be a mere entertainer. She had the run of the ranch and a queen could not have ruled her subjects more regally than Adeline ruled the barnyard. When she waddled up to a feed trough the chickens and ducks stood back respectfully until she had had her fill and waddled away.

"It's a miracle — the way she has them buffaloed," I said after watching one of these performances.

"'Tain't no miracle," Jack said. "I saw what she done to a rooster that wouldn't stand back from the trough. She grabbed him by the neck, hauled him down to the crik and almost drowned him before I could get there."

Completely cowed by the rooster's brush with death, the barnyard fowls scattered at Adeline's approach. Obviously the goose identified herself with the human race until one day in late fall — the day a flock of geese flew over the ranch.

Wezie and I were out in the yard when we heard the wild, sweet clamor of their honking. Looking up, we watched this miracle of precision that was etched against the sky; the wedge of undulating wings that glinted silver in the sun.

As we stood there enchanted, the lead goose fell out of the triangle, seemed to float for a moment, then dropped back to the rear of the flight. Without a wasted motion or so much as an instant's slowing the first goose in the right arm of the wedge took over as leader. It was a strange and awesome sight, something I'd never witnessed before.

I caught Wezie's hand and lowered my voice as I would in church. "I wonder why the leader gave up his place."

"The lead goose falls back when he gets tired," Wezie told me. "Leigh read me about it — in my bird book. You see the leader gets tireder than the geese behind. They protect each other from the wind and he has to take it head-on."

The strange, exciting honks grew louder as the triangle flew over our heads. Wezie nudged me and whispered, "Adeline's looking too." Adeline's head was rigidly erect, her bill uplifted. Suddenly, with no warning, she let out a small, rusty honk. Wezie dropped to the ground and hugged her.

"She's trying to talk to them, Mother. She knows they're her kinfolks."

"You betcha she knows." Jack had come up behind us. "I'd best get some sheep shears and clip her wings right now."

"No." Wezie held Adeline closer and stroked her arched neck. "I won't have her beautiful wings clipped."

"But Jack's right, honey. Adeline will fly away some day if we don't clip her wings."

"If she wants to go," Wezie said slowly, "if she really wants to go, I wouldn't try to stop her."

I realized then that my child, young as she was, had already learned the sad, irrevocable lesson of wild things tamed by man. She knew that sooner or later the goose would leave us.

But Adeline showed no inclination to leave us that fall; and she didn't join her kinfolks in the spring when they flew over the ranch on their way up from the south. I began to wonder if the unnatural goose preferred the little familiar ditches of earth to the uncharted sea of the sky.

Later, I noticed that Adeline didn't sing as much, that she'd lost interest in Patches and seldom ambushed him any more; that she was restless and had taken to wandering up the canyon alone.

She'd be gone less than an hour at first, then several hours, then a whole day. And somewhere in her journeying she must have heard and answered the mystic call of nature, because when the inevitable migration headed south that year she spread her unclipped wings and left us.

We never forgot her. For years, whenever Wezie and I heard a wild sweet honking, saw a flight of geese silver-etched across the sky, we wondered if one of these dauntless voyagers could be our own Sweet Adeline.

Chapter Four

WEZIE STARTED TO SCHOOL the same autumn that Adeline left us. She rode horseback with her brothers to the small one-room district school that was seven miles from our ranch. I'd been dreading it. The rigors of Montana winter were just ahead and from January to March the children would have to be driven to school. This meant that Tom would have to get up before daybreak to thaw out the frozen motor of his car. It meant that one of us would have to shovel snowdrifts that could build up over night to a height of several feet. It meant bitter, lashing wind that took the breath from our lungs and brought tears that froze on our lashes. It meant frostbitten cheeks and hands and feet. Bad enough for two sturdy boys . . . far worse for a little girl.

But by the time October arrived I was glad to see Wezie go to school, to know she'd have the diversion of playmates her own age and kind. She was taking Adeline's departure too hard although she never talked about it as the rest of us did. (We all missed the crazy goose; the ranch seemed a bit dull after Adeline's defection.)

I felt sure Wezie expected her pet to return. For weeks she never rode Patches far and she spent more time than usual in her playhouse. I found her there one morning, standing perfectly still in the middle of the room. There was something about her small straight back that caught my attention as I paused by the door. I saw her fold a beruffled red organdy dress, raise the lid of a trunk and place it carefully on top of the ridiculous baby outfit that Adeline had once clowned in.

Stepping inside I picked up a doll that lay half clothed in a corner. "Poor Miranda, that dress belongs to her, Wezie. Let her wear it again."

"No." Wezie closed the trunk and sat down on it. Her face crumpled and her eyes were bright with unshed tears. "No."

I knelt down beside her. "Oh, honey —"

"Her feathers were so soft, Mother," she whispered, "so — so soft."

I tried to talk to her but that was all she would say. That was all she ever did say about Adeline.

Tom, usually soft spoken, was vehement when I told him. "So help me, this is the last wild thing anybody's going to bring on this ranch!"

"I agree absolutely. Anyhow until Wezie's old enough to accept the fact that they'll all die or desert in the end."

Tom paced the room. "Oh, Lord, if she'd just bawl over that silly goose — or talk about it."

She's like you, I thought. She keeps the things she feels the most inside. I remembered a day when Dolly, Tom's favorite mare, had stepped in a badger hole and broken her leg . . . I came in his office for something and found him loading a gun.

"Porcupine?" I wanted to know.

"Dolly's broken her leg," he said in a too level voice. "I've got to shoot her."

"Oh Tom, you can't! You mustn't! Let one of the men —"

"One of the men might miss," he told me matter-of-factly.

You'd never have known that the big mare wasn't just any horse except that Tom buried Dolly. He didn't leave her carcass for the coyotes and wolves. And he didn't talk about her either.

"She could have kept Adeline," I said slowly. "She could have let Jack clip her wings — Oh, well, the goose is gone and it's up to us to find Wezie another pet. A dog?" I suggested, knowing full well what his answer would be. All dogs on our ranch were young enough to work or old enough to be retired. "A lamb? At least it would stay put."

"You know she wouldn't bother with a lamb."

This was something I'd often puzzled about. With all her love for animals Wezie had never taken to sheep individually. They were her father's business, and in the nature of things came first. As young as she was she knew that they clothed her, fed her and kept her warm, but one sheep to Wezie was the same as another.

"There's this advantage," I insisted. "She'd never get so attached to a lamb that she'd hate to see it go back to the herd."

Tom took a dim view of orphan lambs. They were noisy and stubborn and hardly worth the milk and effort it took to raise them. It wasn't easy to persuade him but he finally agreed to let Wezie have a newborn ewe lamb in the spring. Ewe lambs were no less trouble, but easier to dispose of when grown.

I talked it over with Wezie that night. She wasn't interested. It was Andy, the indefatigable optimist, who became enthusiastic at once. With pencil and paper (and flights of fancy) he showed his sister how she could build up a whole herd of sheep by the time she was grown.

"I don't want a herd," she said. "We've got plenty of sheep already."

Never mind, I thought, I'd bring her a cute, soft little lamb and she'd change her mind. But spring and lambing were six months away and in that time Wezie became adjusted to Adeline's departure. At least she didn't grieve for the goose any more. And she liked school. School would close in June, however, and then our child would be at loose ends and on the lookout for another feckless orphan of the forest. With a pang I remembered the wild creatures we'd adopted over the years — all dead or departed, each taking a bit of our hearts along when they went — and resolved to try to avoid another such experience.

There was more snow than usual that winter and it was middle May before I dared risk my car over the uncharted trail that led to the closest lambing camp. The morning was balmy and warm with patches of snow still scattered like polka dots over the tender new green of the range. I found a level spot to park, turned the car down hill and walked toward a grassy knoll where a herder, with his two dogs, was guarding the "drop band" (lambing ewes). I was out of breath when I reached him.

"Hi!" I panted, waving my scarf.

The herder turned his head slowly, then yanked his hat down over his ears. I'd never seen the man before but this was a familar greeting with herders — an instinctive wariness of "wimmenfolk." Caution was unusually active in this man and with reason. The very next week he was hauled into court for bigamy. However, at the moment, I didn't suspect I was dealing with a bigamist but it might account for the underhand trick he was about to deal me.

"I'm looking for a good whiteface ewe lamb," I told him confidently. "An orphan or twin."

He stared out over his flock, I felt sure to keep from looking at me. I was surplus commodity also to his way of thinking.

Emerging briefly from under his hat he said, "I got orders from the Boss not to give 'bums' away."

"The Boss meant you're not to give them to drifters who'd be traipsing all over the ranch, picking up good lambs they found on the way. I'm the Boss's wife. It's all right to give me a lamb."

"I got my orders," he muttered.

I clenched my fists. "Do I have to bring a note from Tom to get one of our own lambs? Of all things — " I broke off and pointed to two woolly little creatures which were suckling one ewe. "Those twins! Why can't I have one of them?"

I could almost see his hackles rise. "You don't want one of them," he said flatly.

"I certainly do! I want the one on this side. Now, will you please catch it and put it in my car?"

"Nope." He reached down, pulled a long stem of last year's grass and picked his teeth with it.

"Them's rams," he explained after a moment.

"You might have said so sooner." I looked out over the milling herd of blatting ewes. "Don't tell me that in all this drop band there isn't one orphan female lamb."

He eyed me from head to foot, a scowl on his face. Then surprisingly his whole attitude changed. Without a word he snatched up his sheep crook and strode through the flock. He snaked a small struggling creature from its mother's teats and brought it to me.

"This here's a triplet," he said.

Tom didn't even approve of twins. He figured a ewe could suckle a single lamb better than two. What would he say to a triplet? I was trying to think of some way to refuse without antagonizing the herder further when the little thing bleated. I took a second look and that did it.

The triplet was the smallest lamb I'd ever seen. It had an adorable crinkled face, bright round eyes and long knobby legs. It might have just stepped out of a Christmas card. Head cocked on one side the baby thing looked me over. I reached out a hand. It nuzzled hopefully, running velvety lips over my wrist.

"Let me hold her," I said. The lamb was feather light.

"Such a bitsy thing," I rubbed my cheek against a pink-lined ear. "I didn't know they came this small. I think I'll call her Bitsie."

"Better fatten it up before the Boss sees it." The herder reached for another spear of grass. "The Boss don't take to runts."

"I'll fatten her up," I promised. But it wouldn't be for Tom. It would be for Wezie. I didn't want Wezie to see this lamb until she was at her cunning best. I thanked the herder and left.

Tom was gone when I reached the ranch so I drove to an abandoned sheep shed, a quarter mile down the canyon. Wezie seldom rode this way so it would be a good place to hide the lamb until she got some meat on her bones.

I regretted my choice of a home for Bitsie before the first week went by. Four times a day I traipsed to the shed, bottle in hand. Four times back. I must say I was always touched by the heartiness of my welcome. Bitsie quivered with excitement when she saw me coming, poked her small moist nose between the planks that confined her and bleated with unrestrained rapture.

"She's filled out unbelievably," I told Tom at the end of two weeks. "She's begun to look like a regular lamb — on the small side, of course."

Tom eyed me, frowning. "You're beginning to look on the small side yourself. I wish you'd quit all this running back and forth and bring that lamb up to one of the small corrals."

"I will when school closes. I don't want Wezie to see Bitsie until there's time for the two of them to get acquainted." I was looking forward to next week when school would be out, and I could turn my job over to Wezie.

But trouble struck from a completely unexpected direction before I could put my child to the test. Lambing was at its peak now. In spite of my urgings Tom hadn't found time to visit Bitsie. He promised and finally came down to the shed one rainy morning while I was feeding the lamb.

"Wezie's starter herd," I quipped, pulling an empty bottle from Bitsie's greedy mouth.

Tom got down on his knees beside Bitsie, and looked her over carefully. He got up and brushed the hay from his levis. "Your ewe lamb is a ram. He hasn't even been altered."

"Oh, no!" I slumped down on a bale of hay and thought back to the day I'd got Bitsie. Had the herder actually told me that Bitsie was a ewe lamb? No. I'd taken it for granted. "Why would he give me a ram? I told him plainly what I wanted."

"He was passing the buck." I could see the play on words amused Tom. It didn't amuse me.

"Why?"

Tom's face sobered. "He must have skipped this lamb somehow when he brought the rest in to be altered. He had to get rid of him. You just happened to be handy."

"What do we do now?"

"It's a little late but the lamb will have to be castrated. He's no good the way he is."

"No. I won't put him through that." I caught Bitsie protectively in my arms. "Why can't he just stay a ram? Some sheep do."

"Because he's not a purebred. He's a cross between Cotswold and Rambouillet. He can't run with the ewes."

I didn't see why not at his tender age but I didn't argue. "What are we going to do?" I was ready to take Tom's advice until it came.

"Castrate him, and ship him to market with the rest of the lambs. It's all we can do."

"No! I won't let you. You can't!" I looked at Bitsie's loving, trusting, always hungry face and felt sick.

"We've got to get rid of him, Hughie. He'd be dynamite when he's full grown." Tom meant it. When he got that certain tone in his voice I never argued, but I begged him to give me a week. "Maybe I can find Bitsie a good home."

"Nobody wants a crossbred ram, Hughie." Tom's stern face softened. "You can try if you want to. But remember he's got to go — one way or another — by the end of the week."

"Or another" meant Bitsie would have to be altered and shipped with the rest of the wether lambs in the fall. I couldn't bear to think of Bitsie in terms of lamb chops so I hurried back to the house and phoned every small sheep grower in the community. Our telephone bill in the next few days added up to the price of a lamb but nobody wanted Bitsie. Furthermore the story of my deal with the herder had spread out over the party line. The ranchmen eyed me with sidelong glances and could hardly conceal their mirth; the boys teased me. But Wezie was embarrassed over my gullibility.

"Didn't you even look, Mother?" I looked all right but at the wrong end, I thought, remembering Bitsie's adorable, crinkled face and round bright eyes.

Five days of my week went by and I hadn't found a home for Bitsie. Desperate now I called my good neighbor Mrs. Bennetts. She found it hard to understand all the fuss over the disposal of a mere lamb but she came up with a good suggestion.

"Old Mrs. Bailey over near Cameron is boarding a couple of horses and a hunting dog for some dudes, maybe she'd board the ram until you can make other arrangements."

I jumped in my car, loaded Bitsie in the back and drove to the small, dry farm where the widow Bailey lived. She agreed to board Bitsie. She had more milk than she needed and was glad of a chance to pick up some cash. However, she made me inspect her corral before we turned Bitsie into it.

"It's good and tight," she assured me, "but I can't be responsible if your lamb breaks out."

"He won't leave," I laughed. "Not so long as you keep his stomach filled."

Bitsie had a reprieve and I was so relieved that I didn't puzzle over Mrs. Bailey's precautions. I sang all the way home. Tom took it for granted that I'd given the lamb away and I didn't enlighten him. I saw no reason to stir things up by admitting that Bitsie was now a star boarder.

The rest of the summer was a busy one for me. Our cook eloped with one of the men in June, so hurriedly she left her false teeth in a glass of water on a shelf above the sink. They were grinning at me when I came down to take over at four o'clock next morning.

I thought of Bitsie often but didn't have time to visit

him until fall. By then he was a fine, proud ram and his affections had drifted elsewhere. Mrs. Bailey was the one who fed him . . . It made me feel a little sad.

"He looks like a purebred," she boasted then added wistfully, "I always liked whiteface sheep best."

If I'd only presented him to Mrs. Bailey that morning. I toyed with the idea for a moment but decided that such a beautiful ram deserved a more ambitious future. Again I tried to find a permanent home for Bitsie in a Rambouillet herd. I answered ads, wrote woolgrowers in Nevada, Idaho and Wyoming with no luck at all.

Bitsie was suddenly a year old and another summer on its way out. In late August I got a frantic phone call from Mrs. Bailey.

"Bitsie's gone! He's broke out!" she panted, sounding on the verge of tears.

"Don't feel so bad about it —" I began but she wouldn't let me get a word in.

"I didn't know the screws was loose in that corral gate latch. How'd I know he was strong enough to butt a gate down? He's your buck, Mis' Call. You better get some men out to look for him. I ain't responsible. You know I told you that in the first place."

"I'll send someone to find him," I promised and turned away from the phone. Mrs. Bailey was a stolid woman, a woman of few words. She must be mighty fond of Bitsie to get so excited because he was missing. To this day I can't imagine why I didn't guess the truth, how I could have been so stupid . . .

I ran out to the corral for help. No men were around

but Wezie was saddling Patches. "Ride up to the hayfield and get your Daddy," I told her. "Bitsie's lost."

"Daddy's measuring hay. Now Mother, you know he won't quit to look for Mrs. Bailey's lamb."

"Never mind. There's Hank. He can go." The camp tender was leading his horse through the gate and I called, "Don't unsaddle, Hank. Mrs. Bailey's in a stew. Bitsie's broke loose and she wants someone to look for him." Hank had been tending sheep camps all day. He was hot and tired and in no mood to hunt sheep for Mrs. Bailey.

"She's got a nerve!" He undid the cinch on his saddle. "Let her get somebody else to look for her ram." His nice young face suddenly brightened with a wide grin. "Lucky you got rid of that lamb when you did. The way the wool market's falling Tom'd hate to shell out a bundle of cash for out-of-season lambs."

So that was why Mrs. Bailey was upset; that was why she'd forced me to admit ownership of Bitsie over the party line. I understood everything now. Of all the crazy, unpredictable crises in the sheep business this was one I'd never encountered before but it plainly was a calamity.

"I didn't give Bitsie away," I croaked. "He still belongs to me."

"Good Lord!" Hank snapped the cinch buckle back into place, grabbed the reins and leaped on his horse, calling to Wezie. "Ride down for the Boss, kid. I'll find Jack."

They galloped away, leaving me in the middle of a dusty corral in practically a state of shock. Wezie didn't find Tom. He'd gone to town. But a few minutes later

I heard our truck rattle up the hill. When it returned it had another passenger — Bitsie. Bitsie had spent a night in the herd of Mr. Sorenson, a small woolgrower down the road. He had, without doubt, according to Hank, bred a number of ewes which would drop their lambs in freezing weather when they could not hope to survive the winter — lambs which Tom later paid for at current prices and maximum weight. My brief fling in the sheep business cost Wezie and me a month's vacation in Texas, some badly needed winter coats and the three old ewes with which — plus Bitsie — I bribed Mrs. Bailey to become a woolgrower and raise whiteface sheep on her own.

Chapter Five

Two years had gone by since Wezie lost Adeline and
so far there had been no forest orphans to take the goose's
place. Coalie and Midge died of old age in those years and
we now had Bingo, another retired sheep dog, to laze out
his days on the vine-covered porch. Patches had been
jealous of Coalie and Midge as long as they lived but he
tolerated Bingo — because Bingo was a man's dog, I suppose, and followed the ranch hands when he moved around
at all.

The tie between Wezie and the little horse had strengthened, if possible. There was scarcely an hour of the day in
summer when they weren't together. She never left him
in the corral without a quick hug or a kiss on the white
spot between his eyes and he never failed to whinny when
he saw her coming.

I watched Wezie grow taller with a vague sense of foreboding. When I lengthened her dresses it was the stirrups
of her saddle that I thought about. I finally brought my
anxiety to Tom. "What will we do when Wezie gets too
big to ride Patches? When she has to have another horse?"

"Let's cross that bridge when we get to it," Tom said matter-of-factly, but I could tell by the look on his face that he'd been concerned too. I reassured myself with the thought that Patches would be around for a number of years and as long as he was he'd take the place of other pets. I wanted no more enchanting transients from the forest. But I got one when Joe Belden, the ranger, turned up one day with an antelope fawn in his arms. He'd found it under a wild currant bush, not far from the forest, count- ing corrals, he told me, placing the skeleton-thin creature in my arms.

I looked down at the pathetic baby whose soft brown eyes seemed already glazing in death. "What happened to its mother?"

"Struck by lightning, maybe, or killed by some hunter." Joe shrugged. "Might even have been caught in a trap. But I've kept an eye on this fawn since yesterday morning. If the doe was alive she'd have come back to suckle it."

"Poor little thing. Let's see if we can feed her."

Joe cradled the fawn with a surprising gentleness, con- sidering the ham-like size of his hands, and talked steadily while I heated the milk. He told me about a party of geologists "rocking" in the mountains; about the condition of the range — about the late frost that had mowed down most of the valley gardens. I smiled to myself knowing that Joe, with the typical roundabout approach of the native Montanan, was sidling up to some subject uppermost in his mind. I was afraid I knew what that subject was. But he didn't quite get around to it. The milk was warm now.

I kneeled down on the floor and tried to feed the fawn with a spoon but the milk dribbled out of the side of her small lax mouth.

"She's too far gone to swallow, Joe."

"We need to get the milk farther back in her throat," he said. "Got a medicine dropper?"

The medicine dropper was an improvement. The milk still dribbled but I had a feeling that some of it slipped down the delicate throat. The fawn hadn't moved, but now we could see the lift of shallow breath against her ribs.

"We've done all we can," I wrapped the little thing in a scrap of blanket and put her behind the stove. "I'll keep trying to feed her," I promised.

"She may not make it." Joe reached for his hat. "But say, Mrs. Call, I'd appreciate it if you'd keep her a few days till we know."

"I'll do what I can," I assured him, not at all surprised to have an ailing fawn dropped in my lap; only thankful it wasn't a moose or a bear. Our ranch lies between the Forest Reserve and town. Government trappers, rangers and even the game warden had a way of leaving sick or ailing animals with us until they recovered or died.

In the past if the orphans recovered, they became permanent members of the family. The children wouldn't let us send them away. "You've got to come for this fawn the minute she shows any sign of life," I warned hastily. "Before Wezie gets attached to her."

Joe twirled his hat on an oversized finger and said casually, as though the thought had just that second struck him, "Antelopes have got it all over the rest of the deer family — for pets anyway."

There was no longer any doubt in my mind about what Joe Belden wanted.

"I'm not going to be an easy mark this time." My voice sounded waspish and I added in a milder tone, "I'd think you'd be ashamed! After Lady, how could you plot to leave that fawn here permanently?"

Joe looked uncomfortable, clapped his hat down on his sandy hair and left before I could say another word about Lady, a deer which the children had raised. Joe found her, half starved and whimpering near the carcass of her dead mother, years before. He brought her to the ranch. I wasn't yet wise to the ranger's method of preserving ailing wild life entrusted to his care; and I actually urged him to give the fawn to the children.

He agreed, but in leaving threw in an afterthought which turned out to be as cunning as the fine print in an accident policy. "Let her run free," he told us. "It's against the law to pen her up."

We let Lady run free and two years later, when she'd won all our hearts with her gentle ways, she picked up and left us with no more than a flick of her small white tail. It was a tragic experience for the three children. I didn't want them to suffer again.

It took Joe's most recent orphan just one week to recuperate, get herself named and win most of our hearts, especially Wezie's. And this in spite of all my efforts to isolate her from the little girl.

"Oh, Mother, let me feed her," she begged each time a bottle was filled.

Goodness knows it would have been a help to agree. Our current cook was recuperating from an operation in a Butte hospital and we were getting ready for haying. All the extra dishes, packed away in the basement last fall, had to be lugged upstairs, washed and stacked in the pantry. Supplies in the commissary had to be checked. I'd have to spend a whole afternoon in town restocking items that ranged from dried beans to ham.

There'd be no time to shop after haying started. Yet I took precious moments to feed the little antelope, now in the barn. I'd put her there the minute she recovered enough to stumble up on her dainty black hoofs. Mainly because the barn was forbidden territory to Wezie.

"I'm going to name her," Wezie said, tagging along when I set out with the bottle. "It can't hurt just to name her."

"It can't help either," I replied firmly. "I've already phoned Joe Belden to come get her."

"When is he coming?" Worried young eyes questioned me.

"I couldn't reach him," I had to admit. "But I left word with a wrangler. Joe'll be here right away."

"He might not come for several days, so I'm going to name her. I'm going to name her Missie."

"Why Missie?" I looked down on the small overalled figure.

"Because," her voice caught, "I'm going to miss her so much when you send her away."

"Oh, dear Lord," I breathed, feeling like a monster. "Now listen, Wezie. You cannot keep this antelope. I know you think I'm mean and unreasonable but — oh,

honey, remember how you felt when Lady went away?
When Adeline left? This little fawn would grow up and
leave us too and we'd be unhappy all over again."

Probably more so, I thought. The little antelope had
been around just a few days and, lately, Wezie had seen
her only at feeding time. How could she have grown so
attached to her? I discovered how, that same afternoon,
when one of the hay men let the cat out of the bag. Wezie,
instead of roaming the hills on Patches, as I'd believed, was
spending her time in the barn with Missie.

"Oh, how could you?" I scolded, frightened as well as
angry. "You've been forbidden to go in the barn alone.
You might have been kicked by one of the work horses."

"I was careful, Mother," she said, giving me that slow,
disarming smile so much like Tom's.

"Aren't you sorry at all?" I demanded. "I feel very
bad to think you'd deliberately disobey Daddy and
me."

"I'm sorry I made you feel bad, Mother," she told me,
"but I'm not sorry I went to play with Missie. Missie's
lonesome in that big old barn all by herself."

I walked straight to the telephone and called the ranger
station. Joe Belden answered this time. "Your antelope's
come to life. Making friends all over the place," I said
with significant emphasis. "You'll have to come for her.
Right away."

"I was about to phone you," he apologized. "I've found
a home for the fawn. With Jack Worsham and his wife
— those new people who bought the Shepherd place. I'll
try to pick her up tomorrow."

"You'd just better."

But he didn't come the next day and I had to put Missie in the yard because they needed her stall in the barn for work horses. She was getting to be more and more of a problem. She was always hungry now; it was impossible to fill her up. She'd finish one bottle and nuzzle frantically for more. She was empty down to her little black hoofs. And right where Wezie could see her every minute of the day.

"Missie's hungry, Mother. Oh let me give her a bottle," Wezie would beg. "You don't want her to be hungry, do you?"

"She's worse than Bitsie ever was," I'd grumble.

"She can't forget how hungry she got before Joe found her. If you'd just let me feed her —"

But on that score I was adamant. I had never yet let Wezie get her hand on the bottle. I had reason to know the strong tie that comes to exist between one who needs and one who is needed.

"Oh, isn't she cunning, Mother?" Wezie squeezed my hand. "See the darling way she's looking at you. She wants you to pet her."

The little fawn was indeed "cunning." She'd filled out in the past two weeks, her coat had begun to shine, and she had all the winning ways of a playful kitten . . . I clasped my hands behind my back. All was lost if I, too, became attached to Missie.

I phoned the ranger station — desperately this time.

"Gosh, I'm sorry, Mrs. Call," Joe apologized again. "I can't get by the ranch before the last of the week."

"Why can't those people — the Worshams — come for their pet?"

"I thought of that and phoned them. Mrs. Worsham's been under the weather. Jack can't leave her."

"Then I'll deliver the fawn myself. This very day," I told him, my patience exhausted. Perhaps this would be better anyhow. Maybe Wezie would feel better about letting Missie go if she saw with her own eyes that the little thing had a good home. When I turned away from the phone Wezie was standing directly behind me.

"Would you like to go and see Missie's new home?" I asked.

Her eyes reproached me. "Missie loves us, Mother. She won't want to go."

"She'll be happy with the Worshams," I said, convinced that Missie would be happy anywhere so long as she could fill her little stomach several times a day. "There's nothing we can do about it, honey. Joe's given Missie to them. We can't interfere."

Wezie turned away and I felt even worse about matters when she helped me load Missie into the car and climbed in forlornly beside her.

We set out for the old Shepherd Ranch which was on the other side of the river. Wezie held Missie tightly clasped in her arms and was silent until we rolled over the cattle guard that led into the Shepherd Place. Then my child slid over as far as she could and put Missie on the seat between us.

"I'm not going to carry Missie inside," she gulped. "If she doesn't like it there she'll always remember that I was the one who left her. Oh, Mother, how can you do this to Missie? Look at her darling eyes."

I looked and it was almost my undoing. Those soft, limpid, trusting eyes . . . Wezie leaned down and buried her face against the antelope's neck.

"All right, you wait in the car," I said briskly, reached for Missie, stalked up to the door, and knocked. The little antelope nuzzled my wrist for the bottle I'd brought at Wezie's insistence.

Mr. Worsham, a harassed young man in faded overalls, answered my knock. "It was kind of you to bring her," he said taking Missie in his arms. She struggled frantically, walling her eyes. I handed over the bottle. Then the fickle creature began to nuzzle her new owner's hand.

"My wife'll be sorry not to see you," the young man apologized. "She's been ailing ever since we moved to the valley. She feels real miserable today."

"I'll come back another time. My little girl'll want to see how Missie likes her new home. Oh, I forgot — don't feel obliged to call her Missie," I laughed. "She'll soon learn to answer to any other name when a bottle attends it."

"I like Missie." He smiled and stroked the fawn. "We'll call her that too."

We talked for a moment about the proportions of milk and water I'd used for Missie's bottle, then I walked slowly back to the car.

"He's a nice young man," I said, climbing under the wheel. "He and his wife will be good to Missie, so quit feeling bad."

"She'll be home — homesick for us."

"She'll get over it, honey." Remembering the way Missie had quieted down when the bottle changed hands I was more convinced than ever that she'd be content anywhere she could get all the milk she wanted.

Apparently, I was wrong. Ten days later Mr. Worsham called me on the phone with shocking news. Missie was starving. She refused to take a bottle. The last one she'd suckled was the one I'd left when I delivered her to his ranch.

"I've managed to keep her alive on strained oatmeal water," he told me. "But she's down now. She's just skin and bones, Mrs. Call. Unless she takes milk — well, I doubt if she'll last more than a day, two at the most. I thought I should tell you — that maybe you'd want to try —"

"Of course. Oh, the poor little thing —" I was too shocked to think for a second, then I said, "Wrap her up warmly and bring her right over."

"I can't. My wife's taken a turn for the worse and I've got to get her to the hospital right way. I'll leave the kitchen door unlocked. Missie's in the lean-to beyond."

Appalled I planned swiftly. I was preparing supper for twenty hay men. I snatched off my apron, called to Jack and asked him to take over, thankful that Wezie was helping Tom move a sheep camp that afternoon; that the boys were working in the hayfield. There was a possibility that Missie would be dead before I could reach her . . . I took time to fill a bottle of milk to take along, but I'll never know why.

When I reached the old Shepherd place, the garage door was open, the Worsham car gone. I let myself into the

kitchen, and from there to the lean-to. In the half light of
the room, I didn't see Missie at first. But as soon as my
eyes adjusted to the dim interior my heart stood still. That
couldn't be Missie stretched out on an old blanket in a
corner. Not our fat, saucy Missie . . . this small skeleton
with hide stretched over its pitiful ribs?

Blindly, I turned and ran back for the bottle I'd brought,
but Missie was too far gone to take the nipple. I caught
her up in my lap, made a cup of her underlip and squeezed
a few drops of milk in her mouth. It dribbled back in my
hand. I squeezed milk on my fingers and forced them far
back in her throat, repeating this several times. Finally I
felt her swallow . . .

"Please, Missie — dear little Missie," I whispered, "please
—" and tried the nipple again.

A tremor passed over her body . . . I squeezed the nipple gently and after a few moments Missie's lips closed
feebly over the soft rubber and she began to suckle. I
held my breath. Her eyelids flickered. She suckled again,
this time it seemed with more strength.

I knew she shouldn't take too much milk after a long
fast, so I wrapped her snugly in my sweater, carried her
to the car and put her on the seat beside me. Twice on the
way to the ranch I stopped and let her take a swig at the
bottle, and it seemed to me I could see new strength flow-
ing through her with every drop of milk she drank.

She took another half bottle when I got home and this
time I let Wezie feed her. I'd given up. So far as I was
concerned Missie was a permanent member of our family.

"Oh, Mother, I told you she'd be homesick for us. I told

you. And you wouldn't believe me." Wezie was on her
knees beside the little antelope, her eyes bright with tears.
"She just pined away. She missed us so."

I questioned this. But there was certainly no doubt that
Missie was delighted to be home again. In a week she was
on her feet and running all over the place, as hungry as
ever.

"Why would she refuse milk at the Worsham's?" I
puzzled to Tom. "Could their cow have been eating some
weed that made the milk distasteful?"

"For Missie?" Tom scoffed. "That little glutton? She
takes a bottle so fast she wouldn't know what it tastes like."

Missie's hunger strike at the Worsham's remained a mystery for over a month, and then we learned why she had
refused to suckle. To this very day I think of her instinct
with awe and complete amazement. For we learned that
the milk from the Worsham cow was contaminated. The
doctor had finally diagnosed Mrs. Worsham's trouble as
undulant fever. Some strange, mysterious wisdom of the
wild had warned the little fawn not to drink the milk. But
poor Mrs. Worsham, with only human intelligence to
guide her, had not been so fortunate.

Missie soon became the darling of our ranch. Everyone
loved her. The ranch hands always had a tidbit saved from
a meal or a pat for Missie. Tom, who heretofore had taken
a dim view of any four-legged creature which did not pull
its own weight, and had been violently opposed to Missie's
adoption, let her follow him around on his chores and
roared with laughter when she nipped his coattail for attention. Andy and Leigh took her fishing with them; she

accompanied me on mushroom gathering expeditions . . .

Even Patches had an affection for Missie, which was odd and could only be explained by the truth of the adage "Love begets love." Missie loved everyone and refused to be ignored. Again and again I watched her run up to Patches and nuzzle his neck when she caught him grazing. At first he jerked his head back, flattened his ears and took off. "But Missie's winning him over," Wezie told me with shining eyes. "Yesterday he kept his head down and whiffled her ears when she nuzzled him." Missie loved Wezie and Patches best of all. She followed them every time they rode in the mountains. When she was tired or hungry or just plain bored she sought them out. A beautiful friendship and understanding came to exist between the antelope, the pony and the little tow-headed girl.

Sometimes as I watched them together I remembered Lady and thrust back a sense of foreboding. And one morning — the next spring, when the mountain meadows were carpeted with wild flowers — Missie left us too.

Leigh went out to feed her and she wasn't there. All three of the children were heartbroken, sure that Missie would never have deserted them of her own accord; sure she'd been killed or caught in a trap or broken a leg in a badger hole, or at best was lying helpless somewhere in the mountains. For days we combed the countryside for the antelope and found no trace of her.

Then one morning Wezie burst into the kitchen breathlessly, eyes shining. "Missie's back! Mother! Daddy! Missie's back! She's standing up there on that cliff of rocks beyond the canyon."

All of the family and most of the ranch hands who were still at the breakfast table, rushed outdoors. Sure enough our Missie, a sleek young doe, was silhouetted against the sunrise on a distant peak. And there she stood, perfectly still for the best part of an hour just looking down at her old home.

"She'll come back," Wezie said confidently. But that night when the doe had not returned she told me sadly, "Missie doesn't love us any more."

I looked at Andy and Leigh and knew their sorrow was as deep, though being boys they would never admit it.

"Aw, let her go," Andy mumbled. "Who cares?"

"Sure," Leigh agreed. "There's plenty of antelope in the mountains."

But the stark look in both boys' eyes said, "Plenty. But never another Missie."

I tried to comfort them, to explain that Missie had found friends of her own kind. Perhaps a mate. That this was nature's way. Wezie didn't hear a word I said. Her face was still, with a dreadful hurt. "Missie doesn't love us," she had said.

Missie did love us. I had no doubt of it, and it must have been a sad parting for the antelope too, for we saw her several times that summer — in the same spot, still as a statue. As autumn approached she came less frequently, and then for briefer periods. Finally, she came not at all.

But the children, for years, never went out of the kitchen door in the morning without raising their eyes to that distant peak. They loved Missie still. They would love her as long as they lived.

I had been wrong to try to keep them from loving her. For love is never wasted. It is like rain, I thought. Rain falls on the sunbaked earth, evaporates and is gone; but in the process flowers and grass and trees are nourished. And strengthened. And so it is too, with love and the human heart.

Chapter Six

SHEEP PEOPLE ride high or they ride low; there's nothing in between. When wool and lamb prices are good we buy new machinery, paint our houses and barns, trade in our cars and trucks for late models and if there's anything left we take a trip.

If prices are low we draw in our belts and wait out the cycle. We always know that the cycle will end just before we scrape the bottom of the barrel. It always had — until the depression years.

We went into this cycle after two summers of drought. Hay was scarce and tragically high. Lamb and wool prices hit bottom and it cost Tom more to winter a ewe than she would bring if sold.

We cut corners wherever we could. Tom drove himself day and night. The two boys, young as they were, did the work of men in the hayfield. Wezie rode fences and I let our cook go.

But Wezie and I longed to take on more of the load. Other ranch women over the valley were helping out. My child would come home from school with the news that one pupil's mother was raising Belgian hares for the market; another was selling wild currant jelly to dudes. They were weaving rugs, knitting, quilting . . . There seemed no end to their projects. Unhappily, we had waited too long. The most likely enterprises were already taken and duplication, Wezie learned, was frowned upon.

We did a great deal of checking and finally decided that raising turkeys would be our best bet. The demand would be brisk at Thanksgiving, Christmas and New Years, if at no other time. But most important none of the valley women had gone in for turkeys. So far as we knew the only ones, beyond small barnyard flocks, belonged to Mr. Sorenson — the same Mr. Sorenson who owned the ewes that Bitsie had breezed through on that one fatal night. Still smarting from this experience, I felt that competition with our neighbor would be a real joy.

Tom was mending the front gate when we told him about our plan. He heard us out and then said flatly. "You couldn't have picked anything harder if you'd figured a month. You don't know one thing about turkeys."

"We can learn," Wezie said, but I could see she was already a little deflated.

"Not here you can't. We've got the wrong set-up for turkeys. They ought to range, and we live in a canyon. They're gluttons and you'd lose your shirts with grain the price it is. Besides, there's not room for two enterprises on one ranch and if there were, turkeys would be the last things I'd pick."

This convinced Wezie. Wise little girl, she abandoned the scheme right there and galloped away on Patches. I wasn't convinced although Tom put up an argument that covered everything from the never-flagging appetites of the birds to their complete and unbelievable stupidity. Besides, he warned, the poults were delicate and prone to every ailment known to fowl.

"How does it happen then that Mr. Sorenson is able to support a family, even send one son to medical college, on what he makes out of turkeys?" I asked.

"It happens because he's got a wife and two daughters who run their legs off to keep the pesky things alive until they're six weeks old."

"And after that?"

Too late Tom saw his mistake. When cornered he had to admit that, barring accident, the only way you could kill a half-grown turkey was with the axe.

"I can run as fast as the Sorenson women," I said, "and I'm willing to gamble."

"Well —" Tom oiled the gate hinges, snapped the latch shut. "Just remember, I warned you."

He relented somewhat the next day, feeling I suspected a little guilty for trying to discourage my first independent ranch effort, and the motive behind it.

"Get your turkeys from Sorenson," he told me. "And have him send the bill to me."

"I'd rather go it on my own." I still had part of a birthday check I'd got from my father.

Tom looked a little sheepish, and said we'd settle the

finances later, that nobody set turkeys eggs before May anyhow. I was disappointed to learn this, especially after I'd dug up some old farm journals and discovered that each turkey hen could be expected to lay two and sometimes three "clutches" of eggs. Counting the minimum of two "clutches" (with a third as a possible lagniappe) I was dumfounded. No wonder Mr. Sorenson could send a son to college. I had stumbled onto a bonanza!

That was a cold, bitter spring. The wind blew constantly, hurling the snow against fences and buildings to form great drifts. I watched these drifts mount to unbelievable heights and came again to hate the vast, relentless whiteness. (I lived through many Montana winters before I could see any beauty in snow.) And just as I was beginning to wonder if the bare ground would ever show again warm winds drove down the canyon; it started to rain and almost overnight the snow was gone.

I waited impatiently for the road to dry up, and then drove to the Sorenson Ranch. Mr. Sorenson was shoveling manure into a spreader. He ambled over to the corral fence and lounged against it while I explained my mission.

"Tom in on this?" I suspected Mr. Sorenson was remembering Tom hadn't been in on the Bitsie deal until the end.

"He agreed," I said coldly and was ashamed because I suddenly recognized Mr. Sorenson's question for what it was — an odd little quirk of the old-time Montanan who loves to string a deal out, even so small a deal as mine. "Well, how about it?" I asked.

Mr. Sorenson shut one eye, pushed back his hat and

considered. "Look," he advised, "you'd do better to buy eggs and put 'em under chicken hens. Or hatch 'em in an incubator. I got a little one I'll sell you cheap."

"I want three hens and a gobbler," I insisted. "I'll take my turkeys simon-pure. I won't interfere with nature."

"Nature'll interfere with you," he prophesied. But when I said I'd take that chance he reluctantly called his wife, who with the aid of two daughters located and ran down my flock, tied their feet and settled them in the back of my car.

The hens, I was pleased to note, were ladies, resigned to their supine and cramped position. They never once cheeped. But the gobbler thrashed about in an alarming fashion, pecked furiously at his bonds and gobbled. I could almost feel the impact of his wrath against the back of my neck and was relieved when I dropped over the hill and saw the red-roofed buildings of the ranch below.

Tom had just come through the gate in his truck. He waited for me, walked over and looked at my passengers. "Want me to help you unload?"

Since it had never occurred to me that he wouldn't help me unload I replied stiffly, "No, thank you. This is my project."

I glanced into the rear mirror as my car got under way and surprised a gleeful grin on his face. He meant to make it just as hard as possible . . . In a nice sort of way, of course.

I pushed the gas throttle to the floor and bounced into the chicken yard with a speed that sent an old rooster squawking for cover. Getting out of the car I looked my stock in trade over dubiously. They were looking at me too; it seemed in a baleful fashion. Even the hens, whose bright shoe-button eyes stared unblinkingly. I had never touched a turkey which wasn't picked and ready for the oven.

But if I meant to raise turkeys I would certainly have to touch them. Cautiously, I reached for the string that secured the gobbler's feet, figuring it might be smart to let him come out on his own power. He broke into shrill, hysterical gobbles and flapped his crimson wattles angrily. I backed away, returned and reached again. The gobbler reached too and nipped my hand.

Eventually, I was forced to get a gunny sack, hold it over his agitated head, then untie his feet. He exploded from the car with the speed and force of a cannon ball, knocking me flat as he went.

And he never forgave me. Wezie or Jack could walk up to him and he'd turn tail and run, but so long as that gobbler lived I never set foot in the chicken yard that he didn't let out a bloodcurdling war whoop and make straight for me. And even after I'd learned to ward off his attacks with a broom he'd still drag his wing feathers and prance stiff-legged at a safe distance, gobbling his wrath at the top of his lungs.

He seemed to be a necessary evil but at the time I was more concerned with the hens. Mrs. Sorenson had told me I could expect them to start laying their first "clutch" of eggs any day. In anticipation of this event I bought some barrels, sawed them in two and placed them optimistically in the choicest corner of the hen house, dispossessing some Rhode Island Red hens in the process. This invasion made Jack unhappy.

"Turkeys are dumb," he muttered sulkily. "They'll steal the hens' nests and trample their eggs. 'Sall right with me. I don't go for fried chicken like some I know."

He needn't have worried; he knew as little as I about the whims and habits of turkeys. Those hens scorned the deluxe quarters when I herded them into the chicken house and were encouraged by the gobbler who strutted outside, gobbling his derision.

One by one I shooed the hens into the barrels, hoping to familiarize them with their new surroundings. And one by one they looked the premises over with the disdain of a tony matron inspecting a slum and stalked away. For more than a week I shut them in every morning and didn't turn them out until afternoon. I never found an egg and there came a day when I couldn't find a turkey hen.

I searched in secret for a week, through sheep sheds, granary, barns and corrals. Wezie, bless her, spent hours on Patches trying to locate nests in the canyon, and never once reminded me that I'd been warned I'd have trouble. Tom didn't remind me either but he was watching my activities with ill-concealed glee. I finally confided in Jack.

"They're up the crik," he told me smugly. "I saw one under those bushes just past the bend." He didn't offer to help me bring them home. Considerably dashed, I raced up the creek, through brambles and brush and twisted, low-hanging willows; was forced to wade several times because the willows were so thick I couldn't squeeze my way along the bank.

The first (and only) nest I discovered was a good half mile from the ranch and I shouldn't have found it if my hair hadn't tangled in a gooseberry bush which a turkey hen had chosen for shelter. I jerked a flowering branch and there she sat, regarding me with the blank, lackluster eyes of a sleep walker.

"I'll fix you, Madam," I threatened, making a poke of my apron. "Once I get your eggs back where they belong I'll lock you in until they're hatched."

When I thrust out a hand and tried to reach under her she came to life with an angry cluck and defended her eggs with beak and claw. Defeated for the moment, I backed away. She settled down to her dreams again. I sneaked around to the rear and tried once more. This time she drew blood. Sucking an injured finger, I found a stick and poked it under her. She sat tight and I broke an egg. Discouraged and remorseful now, I left her and decided to search for the other nests. I couldn't find one, though I hunted at least an hour longer.

When I finally emerged from the willows I looked a sight. My dress was caked with mud and torn; my hair stood out like a brush. Tom was standing in the door of the blacksmith shop.

"Been looking for something?" he called out solemnly.

"Not a darn thing." I sailed past him and into the house.

As quickly as I could shower and dress I drove to the Sorenson Ranch. Mr. Sorenson was mending a fence.

"What am I going to do?" I wailed after relating my story.

"I warned you you'd best set eggs under chicken hens," he reminded.

"But you didn't tell me that turkey hens would sneak off and hide their nests where Houdini couldn't find them and fight like wild cats if you tried to take the eggs."

"You didn't ask me," he replied with the maddening logic of the Montana rancher who, I eventually learned, will give you advice but once and then unembellished by the reason why.

"I'm asking you now. Suppose I can't make those hens come back to the chicken house?"

His mustache twitched. "No need to suppose. You can't."

"Very well. The nests being where they are, I'd like to know just what to expect."

"Well," Mr. Sorenson popped his galluses thoughtfully, "say the weasels and skunks don't eat all the eggs — I'd give the poults that hatch a fifty-fifty chance with the coyotes." He was optimistic as it turned out.

Meanwhile, back at the ranch the gobbler was strutting about the chicken yard eating his head off. I certainly had no use for him and when all hope of recovering the rest of my flock was gone I telephoned Mr. Sorenson and asked if he wouldn't like to buy him.

"I got no use for a Tom," he replied. "Whyn't you eat him?"

"Eat him!" I yelped. "I'd as soon eat a tiger."

"Your men won't have no such scruples," he opined and hung up.

I decided he was right and next Sunday I baked my old enemy for dinner, feeling I was taking a mean advantage because for once I had him where he couldn't fight back. Scraping plates after the meal I said to Tom, "Well — here goes the last of a promising business."

I was wrong although I didn't find out until early September. It had snowed in the night, a heavy, wet snow. I was taking some laundry off lines in the yard when I heard a familiar "cheep."

Oh, no! I thought and jerked around to see the three lost hens mincing along in the snow with six gangling offspring in their wake. They were heading for the grain troughs in the chicken yard. I left a suit of Tom's frozen underwear dangling weirdly by a sleeve and raced out the gate. Jack beat me to the chicken yard and the turkeys beat him. All nine were crowding greedily around the trough.

"They must of been grazin' in the upper wheat fields," Jack told me. "Snow made the pickin' poor so they hi-tailed it to the house. It's like I said — "

Only part of my mind heard his gloomy predictions. The rest was concerned with a sum in subtraction. The gobbler had proved what an unbelievable amount of grain one turkey could eat. He had furnished a meal for the men and partially paid his way. But *nine* such appetites! I couldn't swing it. Tom was short of grain, already planning to buy corn and cottonseed cake to winter his ewes. I'd have to see if Mr. Sorenson would take the flock off my hands.

But Mr. Sorenson, it seemed, was short of grain too. Furthermore he was getting ready to deliver a load of straw and in a dither to be off.

"I'll sell them cheap," I coaxed after he'd given me one flat refusal.

I'd said the magic word. He thought he might take them when I named the price.

"On a trade, you understand. Come spring I'll give you four settings of eggs for the whole nine of them."

This was a disappointment of course, but would be a relief as well if he'd take them right away. I inquired cagily.

"Well now." He was cagier still. "I make a practice to pay as I go. Seein' as I won't have any eggs to trade until spring you'd best keep 'em at your place."

I stood firm and he finally agreed to let me deliver the turkeys the next day.

I had the winter to think over the deal and failure was a worm in my soul. No matter how I figured it I'd paid good money into Mr. Sorenson's coffers and all I could hope to get back was four settings of eggs.

"Write off your loss and forget it," Tom advised.

I couldn't forget it. I brooded over my loss and finally decided to set the eggs under chicken hens and recover what I could.

"There'll be practically no expense at first," I reminded Tom. "The chicken hens have to be fed anyway. And Mr. Sorenson owes me those eggs."

"Grain's higher than a cat's back," was Tom's cryptic and only remark.

In mid-May I brought the turkey eggs home and set them under four chicken hens. The hens settled down with stolid content and between them hatched out forty poults. If only someone had told me what lovable, friendly little balls of fluff those young poults would turn out to be — had warned me not to make pets of them — but nobody did. I came to love them dearly and unfortunately they came to love me too.

Whenever I walked through the gate, they raced from all directions to eat from my hand, to perch on my shoulders. They followed me everywhere. If I sat down outdoors the whole flock rushed me — to peck at my cheeks, my hair, my hands. Even the sound of my voice brought them running. There came a time when I never dared speak above a whisper if I started for town lest they get under the wheels of my car.

This affection amused and charmed me so long as the poults were small. But they presently shot up into lean, gangling fowls. They couldn't understand why I no longer laughed when they caught me off guard and rushed me in a body or why I fought them off. When it became necessary for me to carry a stick to convince them that I meant business they'd stand in a semi-circle, stupidly craning their necks, peeping forlornly.

These turkeys had but two aims in life; to fill their craws, to be near me. When I shut myself in the yard to weed flower beds they'd run frantically up and down outside the woven wire fence, thrusting their scrawny necks between the wire in an effort to break through.

As soon as their wings developed sufficiently they found a way. They sailed over that six foot fence like a breeze but their flying apparatus, it seemed, only worked one way. They couldn't sail back. A dozen times a day I was forced to drive them out of the gate and the moment I went in the house they'd be in the yard again, peeping expectantly at the back door.

Furthermore they presented a solid front at feeding time and drove the chickens away from the troughs. My relations with Jack became strained; we were scarcely on speaking terms.

I met Mr. Sorenson coming out of the post office one day and confided my troubles.

"You got to teach those turkeys to range," he said. "So long as they can stuff themselves from a trough they won't do nothin' but hang around and pester. Herd 'em up on that flat above your house and make 'em stay till they get their fill of grasshoppers."

Next morning I herded the turkeys to the top of the hill that flanks our kitchen and washhouse. I had no trouble coaxing them up but when I tried to sneak back they came along too. I bowed my neck, trudged up that steep, boulder-ridden hill and rode herd on them for several hours a day but a week passed before they began to appreciate the grasshoppers. And then came a day when I slipped down the hill and not a turkey followed.

"It'll be clear sailing from now on," I boasted to Tom as we sat down to lunch. It might have been, too, if later that afternoon I'd remembered not to shout his name when I called him to the telephone.

My voice was still echoing down the canyon when I heard an all too familiar commotion just over the brow of the hill. I was furious because I'd forgotten how far a voice could carry in this high, thin air but the worst I expected was a prompt return of my pets and another climb to the top of the hill for me.

Suddenly, as I stood there listening, the side of the hill seemed to split wide open. There was a frenzied rush of wings and then, to my horror, I saw the landscape turn black as the turkeys, forty strong, descended. Some by wing and some by foot, but all in a mad, blind rush.

A boulder, which Jack had propped against a rotting telephone pole until he found time to set it, caught the vibration, bounced into the air and went straight through the kitchen window. Another crashed to the roof of the washhouse. Pebbles rained like hail against the side of the house. A dull, ominous impact was followed by the ping of broken wires and I dodged just in time to miss the telephone pole as it hurtled across the fence and landed on the driveway with a dozen turkeys under it.

In the meantime the survivors, completely callous to the fate of their less fortunate kin, sailed over the fence and crowded about me. I drove them off and stumbled across the drive to the side of the washhouse, dreading what I should see. Several of my pets were weaving around groggily but the ones which had hit the log wall head-on were piled on the ground in a limp, still mass of blood and feathers.

Weak-kneed and sick, I slumped down on the kitchen steps. I had only time to take a deep breath before a cyclone of turkeys were on me. Catching me in an old, familiar posture they made the most of it — fighting for the coveted position on my shoulders, their wings raking my face, tangling in my hair. Half smothered, I fought them off, tried to stand up, missed the top step and sat down hard in a flower bed. Before I could rise I felt a hand on my shoulder and Tom plucked me bodily away from my pets.

When the casualties were counted I came out of my venture with fifteen turkeys. The way I felt, that was fifteen too many. I didn't have to go to Mr. Sorenson this time. He heard of the disaster and came to see me. When he appeared I was nursing a black eye, a face full of wing scratches and a lame back in a sunny corner of the living room. Surprisingly, he got right down to business.

"I got a bigger order than I can fill come Thanksgiving," he said. "Like to have me take over what's left of your flock?" Before I could eagerly agree he cleared his throat and added, "On a trade, you understand. Next spring — "

"Oh, no, you don't!" I leaped to my feet, my lame back forgotten. "Don't talk turkey to me! Just take them away. For free. But take them quick."

Mr. Sorenson took me at my word and never mentioned turkeys to me again. But being an independent as well as understanding man, he paid his debt left-handedly. For fifteen years, just before Christmas, he sent me a prime mountain turkey. All picked and ready for the oven — the way he knew I liked turkey best.

Chapter Seven

DOGS ON THE Call Ranch were seldom pets. They were working partners, treated with respect and understanding. Even Wezie, with her passion for animals, learned early that dogs were an important part of the sheep business and that puppies, no matter how cunning and lovable, would have to go out with the flocks as soon as they were old enough to be trained.

A good sheep dog is indispensable to a herder. For one thing a dog can run three times as fast as a man and he frequently averts catastrophies that only the lunatic ingenuity of sheep could devise. A dog discourages bears and coyotes that stalk the herd in the lambing season, holding off marauders until the herder can get to his gun. He saves his master many a weary, footsore mile of walking every day. So the dog is second in importance only to the sheep.

We came by our four-footed partners in two ways. We either bought them as puppies or permitted the herders to use their own dogs. Strays were few and far between in the high sheep country. We never had but one and that one was dumped at our gate.

An irrigator, changing dams in a wheat field that flanked the country road, witnessed the stray's arrival and told us about it at breakfast. He'd watched a car slow down and then take off in a hurry. When the dust cleared he saw a dog racing after the car and losing ground by the minute.

"The pore critter finally gave up and come back, tongue hanging out and limping. I whistled but it ducked under the gate and took out over the hill." The man looked at Wezie, choked back an oath and went on. "I'd like to get my hands on the driver of that car. Anybody that'd dump a dog so far from a ranch house had ought to be hung!"

I looked at Wezie too, saw a familiar, troubled expression shadow her face and wished again that this child of ours would not take unto herself all the woes of the animal kingdom. I wasn't surprised, right after breakfast, to find her wrapping sandwiches in the kitchen.

"Where are you off to now?" I knew the answer before she told me she was going to look for the abandoned dog.

"Not alone," I said firmly.

"Leigh's going too."

I watched them ride off on Patches and Major — the little girl with flying blonde hair and her tall, equally blonde brother. Now Wezie is going to be upset until that dog is found, I thought, put out with the irrigator for talking about the stray in front of her. Just the same I was haunted all morning by the specter of a small deserted animal lost in the mountains.

Wezie and Leigh found no trace of the dog although they rode most of the day. But Jody, one of our herders, discovered it bedded down with his sheep the next morn-

ing. Months later the herder told me about it. When he
whistled the dog had come to him with an ingratiating
wriggle of her thin, shaggy body, had licked his hand and
laid down at his feet. "And that's how I got stuck with
her," Jody confessed.

He'd named her Fidget. I saw the dog at a distance once
that spring when Wezie and I rode up to take Jody some
snuff. She was a long-haired mongrel with the soft eyes of
a doe, the tough feet of a shepherd and the heart, we were
to learn — the big unfathomable heart — of a collie. The
perfect combination for a sheep dog. Unfortunately, she
was also a female and she didn't know when she applied for
a job that female dogs were taboo on our ranch.

The herder knew — and why. Even the children knew
that a working dog will stick to his sheep through thick and
thin, never desert a flock except when he's abused by a
cruel herder or when something tells him that a bitch is
in season within a radius of fifteen miles. Under either of
these circumstances he'll light out for other parts — irre-
sponsible as a hungry, ownerless hound.

Jody knew that he'd more than likely lose his job if the
Boss found out he was working a female and he might have
sent Fidget down to the ranch if the camp tender had
shown up that week. But Hank had an ulcerated tooth.
It was badly infected by the time he reached the dentist
and he had to stay in town for treatment — which made
him four days overdue at Jody's wagon. Those four days
were Jody's undoing. In that short interval Fidget en-
deared herself to him in so many ways that he couldn't
bear to lose her.

And Fidget couldn't have turned up at a better time. Jody was short of help. The week before, his younger dog had tangled with a porcupine. There had been no possible chance of removing the quills from the suffering animal's tongue and throat. Poor Jody had been forced to shoot him, was still upset about it and not looking forward to training another pup.

Fidget needed no training and was a far better helper than Blue, the remaining male dog. Though fully trained Blue had not yet developed that sixth sense which warns of danger before danger occurs. Fidget had this perception to an astonishing degree. She anticipated the adventurous mood of a lead sheep and turned him back just before a dozen or more ewes got a notion to follow. She never had to be sent to round up lambs which loved to nap against sunbaked rocks. When it was time for the herd to move she nosed the lambs out on her own, wakened them gently so they wouldn't take off in every direction, and drove them back to their mothers. She was gentle with the ewes, too, but also firm. They knew she meant business when her sharp bark cautioned them not to go down in a gully or too far out on the ridge of a high cliff. But they weren't afraid of her. Somewhere deep down they sensed she had their best interests at heart.

And the little stray didn't have a lazy bone in her body. Blue frequently resorted to the time-old dodge of weary sheep dogs; pretended he had a thorn in the pad of his paw when he got too hot or tired or bored. He went through a regular routine to gain the herder's sympathy. First he'd limp or run on three legs. Then he'd stretch out on the ground and lick his injured paw and roll his eyes back at his master. Since a lame dog is no good in a sheep camp the herder usually gave him the benefit of the doubt. But Fidget never played tricks, never laid down on the job. And she was as affectionate as a puppy. She loved the sheep and she loved Jody — in that exact order.

Jody was torn between duty and a mounting love for the small, shaggy mongrel. He decided not to be hasty — to give the matter of Fidget's disposal another week's consideration. He watched for Hank's arrival through his binoculars and when he sighted the buckboard and team coming up over a rise, he promptly herded his sheep to such a distance from the wagon that Hank, with four more camps to tend and in a hurry, just left his supplies and didn't bother to look Jody up.

But Hank came a day ahead of time the next week and surprised Jody. He saw Fidget working the sheep and doing such a superb job that he was curious and asked all sorts of questions about "him." Jody claimed he'd bought Fidget from a trapper. Herders frequently work their own dogs, subject to the woolgrower's approval, so Hank thought nothing of this and left the camp relieved to know he didn't have to locate a second dog.

So well did the herder keep Fidget's secret that Tom first learned her sex after the sheep had gone to the Forest Reserve for the summer. An irate woolgrower drove by our ranch and reported that half the sheep dogs of the Forest were now congregated on our allotment.

"Thought you didn't work bitches," he accused.

"I don't," Tom replied.

"Well, you're sure as hell using one now. And you'd better send up a replacement and get her off the Forest or there won't be a dog on any allotment but yours."

"You're barking up the wrong tree."

"I am not. The bitch is a long-haired mongrel and that Jody feller has her."

Tom, the children and I had been loading the car with tackle, provisions and sleeping bags, making ready to start on a two-day fishing trip. Instead we piled into the truck and set out for the Forest Reserve. Tom had a way of clamping his jaw and keeping quiet when something angered him. Wezie tried to make him talk and when she got only "yes" and "no" in reply she giggled and whispered to me, "Daddy's mad because Fidget's popular."

That set us all to laughing; and by the time we'd driven the twenty-six miles (straight up) to Jody's camp — and four more miles before we located him — Tom was in a much better frame of mind. Which was lucky for Jody.

The two dogs were turning the sheep from the rim of a narrow ravine and we stopped the truck until they brought the flock around. None of us had ever witnessed so fine a piece of footwork as Fidget put on that day. She was like a streak of lightning, here one moment, there the next; barking shrilly at obstinate ewes, turning lambs with a gentle nudge on their woolly rumps. Back and forth she raced with a joyous abandon.

The two boys climbed out of the back of the truck to watch and Andy said, "Fidget takes six steps to Blue's one."

"Whew!" Tom whistled, when all danger of a pile-up

was over. "No wonder Jody wants to hang on to her. She just about halves his work."

Jody came toward us now, grinning sheepishly. He was a short, baldheaded man and his thick-lensed glasses gave him the look of an amiable owl.

"If you've come to send me down the road," he said, "the little dog goes too. She belongs to me."

"You know darn well you had no business bringing a bitch to work with my sheep." Tom was stern and Jody sobered.

"Fidget's the best sheep dog in Montana," he defended. "She knows what's what before I do." He pointed. "Who'd suspicion there was a ravine over yonder, all growed up and hid with currant bushes? But Fidget knew. We'd of had a pile-up for sure and lost mebbe a hundred ewes if she hadn't got round first and turned them back."

It was true and there was no disputing it. The little dog had really averted what could have been a major disaster. Tom lit a cigarette, broke the match in two and flipped it to the ground. Then he smiled wryly. "The fact still remains, Jody. You can't work that bitch on my ranch. Now what are you going to do about her?"

"I figure she's already been bred — " the herder began.

"I'll say she has," Tom declared grimly, "by half the sheep dogs on this Forest."

"But look, Boss," the herder wheedled, "she's already done all the harm she can do. There ain't a male dog, except Blue, been around today. So whyn't you let me work her till her puppies come?"

"Then what?"

Fidget raced up and stood beside Jody, licking his hand. The herder sat back on his heels and stroked her small shaggy head. "When the pups come," he said slowly, "you can take her away. I won't say a word."

"Well—" Tom hesitated and I could guess how his mind was working. Puppies were scarce on our ranch at the time; that was why Jody's young dog had not been promptly replaced. Pups are important to the woolgrower. When taken to a sheep camp, each "youngster" learns the intricacies of the most baffling business in the world from an older dog, then replaces him when old age overtakes the veteran, and in turn trains a younger dog. It's an endless circle. Fidget was outstanding. She was new blood, too. Her puppies would very likely inherit some of her courage and ingenuity ...

"O.K.," Tom agreed. "The dog can stay but on one condition. Give me your word you'll let her go — with no more shenanigans — as soon as her pups are born."

Jody agreed and would no doubt have kept his word if little Fidget had been a natural mother. But she wasn't. Her pups came in due course, eight of them. Jody stood by silently the morning the camp tender came to take Fidget back to the home ranch. He wouldn't help but he didn't interfere either — even when the little dog whimpered pitifully and pulled back every time Hank tried to settle her in the buckboard.

"I loaded the pups first," Hank told me when he got back to the ranch, "thinking she'd hop right up with them. But not her. She jumped down and ran smack to the sheep. I had to tie her to the buckboard seat. I got her tied up in the tack room now, and I'll not turn her loose till she mothers those pups."

He turned Fidget free on the fourth day. Next morning she was gone. The puppies, their eyes barely open, were wobbling around on the hay-strewn floor, squealing like little pigs. It was easy to see they'd had nothing to eat that day. Hank asked Wezie to warm some milk and bottle feed them; then he saddled a horse and set out for Jody's camp.

Jody claimed he hadn't seen Fidget so Hank looked no more, figuring the little dog had gone hunting on her own and got killed by coyotes or bears. Otherwise, she'd have shown up at one end of the line or the other.

"It's just as well," Tom told him. "I wouldn't want her around once her pups were weaned."

"Somebody might have wanted her," I said tartly, irked at this continued belittling of the female sex. "All sheep-men aren't as prejudiced as you."

Tom grinned. "That's something we can quit worrying about."

And in the days that followed nobody worried about Fidget except Wezie who had the job of feeding her pups. "How could she leave them, Mother?" she asked me again and again. And one day she added softly, "They're so darling and roly-poly."

"Not *too* roly-poly and darling, Wezie," I warned. I'd been opposed to her feeding the pups; she'd persuaded Tom.

"Now Mother, I know I can only borrow the puppies. But they *are* roly-poly and darling and I just can't see how Fidget could have left them."

"Forget Fidget, can't you, honey? It doesn't help to worry about her."

We didn't forget Fidget — the puppies reminded us — but we never expected to see her again. We probably wouldn't have seen her if a near fatal illness hadn't over-taken Jody that winter.

A storm had been threatening for several days and I'd been hoping it wouldn't break until the weekend when the children were safe home from school. Dun-colored clouds rode low in the sky and a peculiar haze hugged the moun-tains behind the ranch. Around noon Saturday the blizzard struck. The wind reached a shrieking, howling violence and suddenly we were blanketed in snow.

By late afternoon we couldn't see the woodshed which was only a few steps from the kitchen door. The men fought their way to the house for supper, hunched over and so smothered in snow they looked like polar bears. By morning the drifts had piled against the house until they completely covered some of the downstairs windows.

"I've got to get to Jody's camp," Hank fretted at break-fast. "He was half sick with a cold last week and even if he was well he couldn't handle those sheep in this kind of a blizzard — with one dog anyhow."

Tom put down his coffee cup. "How come just one dog?"

Hank shrugged. "Jody didn't want another. Said Blue was enough." He reached for his sheepskin coat. "I better get moving."

"No. You couldn't make it, even on horseback," Tom said firmly. "You'll have to wait till the wind dies down."

It was midmorning before the fury of the storm abated. What had been an impenetrable curtain of snow thinned to a veil. It was now just a matter of slugging through drifts and still, bitter cold.

Hank decided to chance it and left on horseback for Jody's camp. At three o'clock he came galloping back, white under his tan and badly shaken, with the news that he'd found Jody in a fireless wagon, desperately ill and delirious; Blue was in camp but the sheep were nowhere in sight. Hank couldn't move Jody so he'd built up the fire, made him as comfortable as possible and rushed back for help.

In twenty minutes Andy, Leigh and Jack had put a mattress and blankets in the buckboard and were on their way to rescue Jody. I telephoned the doctor who agreed to come as far as the gate on the county road and wait there to take the herder on to town. Tom, Hank and the rest of the ranch hands set out on horseback to look for lost sheep.

Just before dark the wind came up again hurling the snow so that it was impossible to see more than a few feet ahead. Tom and Hank, riding together, gave up for the day and turned back toward the ranch. The chances are they would have failed to hear a distant yapping if Tom hadn't dismounted to tighten the cinch on his saddle. They listened, lost the yapping, then heard it again. Hank had said Blue was in camp . . . Puzzled they rode toward the sound.

In the fast-gathering dusk they topped a rise and saw a small form racing toward them, black against the snow. It was Fidget. As if she knew they had seen her the little dog wheeled and raced back down the hill. They followed and a moment later heard the muted clank of a sheep bell. Then they came on the sheep, bedded down under an overhanging cliff of rocks, so close together they looked like giant drifts of snow. At their approach, a bellwether lurched to his feet and took off. Fidget yapped shrilly and turned him back.

"She must have been turning them back all night," Tom's voice had a note of awe when he told me about it, "the sheep would have been scattered to hell and yonder if she hadn't."

"Where did she come from? Surely Jody couldn't have hid her from Hank for four months."

"Jody's the only one to know that and I doubt if he'll be talking for awhile."

But Jody was made of sterner stuff than Tom figured. He'd been moved to a Butte hospital, survived the trip and was sitting up in bed when I came to visit him a few days later. The first thing he asked was, "Where's Fidget, Mis' Call?"

"She's at the ranch," I told him, smiling. "Quite the heroine. Wezie will have her spoiled rotten before you get out of here." I sobered now. "We're all spoiling her. Even the Boss has forgiven her for being a lady. He's grateful as anything to that little dog for saving his sheep."

Jody brightened. "Reckon he won't be sore now because I kept her. Mis' Call, I didn't lie to Hank when he come hunting her that day. She didn't show up till next morning. What could a feller do when she come back? Come right back and left her puppies behind. What would you of done?"

I wanted to say that I wouldn't have given Fidget up in the first place but, of course, I couldn't say that, being the Boss's wife.

"I had to let Hank take her that day," Jody punched his pillow with a weathered fist. "Lord God, 'twas the hardest thing I ever done in my life. If you could of seen her pulling back, looking so reproachful, like she was asking, 'Why're you sending me off? Didn't I do a good job herding for you?' She — " Jody's voice trailed away. He sank back on the bed.

My sympathies were beginning to run away with me so I broke in practically. "With all her virtues I must say Fidget was a darn poor mother."

"*No Ma'am*, Fidget's smart. She knew you folks'd look after those puppies. Besides some sheep dogs is like that. Sheep comes first with them. It's in their blood, Mis' Call."

"How did you hide her from Hank all that time?"

Jody grinned and raised himself on an elbow. "She hid herself. Ever' time she heard the buckboard coming she lit out and didn't come back till the team and wagon was clean out of sight. Fidget hadn't forgot it was Hank tied her and took her away from the sheep."

I listened to Fidget's virtues for a few minutes longer, then took my leave. "Take good care of Fidget, I'll be back on the job in a few days," Jody said.

We kept Fidget for two weeks — until Jody came to claim her. Then Tom gave the herder a generous bonus. "I ought to give it to Fidget," he said. "Anybody as deceitful and onery as you don't deserve extra pay."

A gleam flickered in owlish eyes behind the thick-lensed glasses. "You already give it to her," Jody said. "Know what I'm going to do with the 'time' I got coming? And my insurance? And this here check?" He grinned. "I'm going down to my homestead in Idaho. Buy me a few ewes and set Fidget up in the sheep business."

And that was exactly what he did. Thus did we dispose of our lady dog. Of course in doing so we lost a good herder.

"Like cutting off your head to cure a cold," Tom observed dourly.

But we profited by the deal, too, because the litter of puppies that Fidget had so callously deserted became veteran sheep dogs which worked out their time and were eventually retired to comfortable old age at the home ranch.

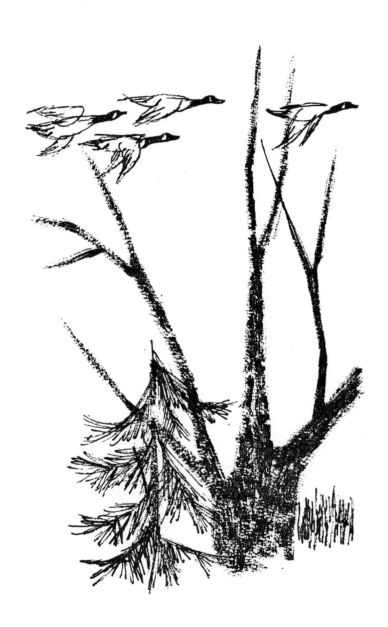

Chapter Eight

ANDY AND LEIGH went away to school the September Wezie was ten. This posed a problem for us. We couldn't let the little girl ride those seven miles without her brothers and the task of driving her back and forth twice a day for the full school term was more than either Tom or I dared take on.

"Couldn't you teach her at home?" Tom asked.

"Are you crazy?" Then I saw he was grinning. I couldn't even add a shearer's tally and get a right answer the first time around and well Tom knew it.

He suggested renting a house in Ennis, the nearest town. "You could come home on weekends from there."

I wouldn't consider this and when Wezie heard she flatly refused. Tom hadn't been sold on the plan anyhow. He missed the boys as it was. And to lose the rest of his family . . .

There seemed only one thing to do. We moved an old log homesteader's cabin from up canyon to a level place on the creek bank, converted it into a schoolroom and hired a tutor.

Wezie was jubilant. She liked Mrs. Buell, a young ex-schoolteacher we'd been lucky enough to find; she liked having school at the ranch mainly because it gave her more time with Patches. This was the last year she would ride the little horse. She must have known that soon she'd be too tall for a pony but she never talked about it and Tom and I, two arrant cowards, couldn't bring ourselves to discuss it with her.

A herder finally brought the situation into the open. He had driven his sheep to the home ranch in December to have them "eyed" (wool clipped away from their eyes so they wouldn't become blind). Wezie rode past the house on her way to the corral just as he came through the gate for supper.

"Hi, kid!" he shouted. "Better trade in that overgrown jackrabbit for a real horse before your heels start draggin'."

She pretended not to hear but I saw her back stiffen. The herder opened his mouth to shout again. "Don't!" I hissed from the steps, then told him a little about it.

"Lord God!" he said, "I wouldn't of made that kid feel bad for anything," and was so remorseful that he made matters much worse by trying to patch them up. When Wezie slid into her place at the table a few minutes later he eyed her and said, "Gosh, kid, you ain't growed a inch since I seen you last."

Wezie was buttering a roll. She dropped a knife on her

plate, pushed back her chair, and said sharply, "I've grown three inches in two years!" Then seeing the herder's distress a little smile replaced the scowl on her face, "Everybody grows," she said.

But it didn't make so much difference to everybody, I thought with a pang. As long as two years ago she must have faced the stark truth — that the time was coming when she'd have to quit riding Patches. Later, when I found graduated marks on the tack room door — where she'd measured, kept track — I was sure.

That night I went downstairs to latch a banging screen and as I came past Wezie's room I thought I heard the sound of muffled sobbing. I opened the door, tiptoed to the bed and bent over.

"Wezie."

She flung both arms around my neck and buried her face against my shoulder, "Oh, Mother! Why do people have to grow? Why can't they always stay the same?"

"Honey — " She wouldn't listen.

"The herder was right! He was right! My heels *will* be dragging soon. And how can I tell Patches? He'll think I don't love him when I ride another horse. Oh, Mother!" Her voice caught on a strangled sob. "Patches lost Missie . . . and if he loses me . . . he'll think nobody loves him . . ."

"You can never tell, honey. Maybe he'll like your new horse."

"I don't want another horse," she said fiercely. "I don't. I don't."

"You've got to have another horse, Wezie. You'd be

unhappy if you couldn't ride with Daddy. He'd be un-happy too."

This got through to her. She worshipped her father. She lay still and silent in my arms, and gradually her sobs subsided the way they had when she was a tiny girl.

"Now," I pushed the hair from her eyes and held her closer, "let's try to figure out how we can manage this thing — there's always a way, Wezie."

We talked for a long time and there in the night in the dim enclosure of that small room the gate of her little kingdom swung open for me and it didn't seem strange to be planning how to bring another horse on the place with-out hurting Patches' feelings.

In the end we decided that the horse would have to be bought soon so that Patches could grow used to him, per-haps make friends, before the inevitable change. She could ride Patches another year . . . She was slight . . . There was plenty of time — it was good to have things settled.

"But you'll talk to Daddy — get him to look around? You won't put it off, Wezie?"

She lay back, pulled the covers up about her neck and kissed me good night. "I'll talk to Patches first," she said.

Next morning she put a handful of cube sugar in her levis pocket and disappeared. When she came back around noon she was walking the pony, her fingers laced in his mane. After that I noticed she spared Patches whenever she could; she seldom rode him high in the mountains; she never jumped him, or raced him along the flat above the house.

"You've got to get busy and find her a horse," I told

Tom. "She's got a notion she'll injure Patches' back if she rides him more than short distances. We can't have her roaming over the mountains on foot."

This built a fire under Tom and a few days later he told us about a horse he could buy. "He's a palomino, Wezie. One of the Cummings string. Want to ride over to Corral Creek this afternoon and see him?"

"All the Cummings' colts were sired by Golden Crevice," I reminded Wezie, thinking the matter was settled then and there. She'd seen Golden Crevice, a splendid animal, in horse shows and parades and admired him extravagantly. So I was surprised to hear her say, "I don't want a palomino."

"Now Wezie, you promised to cooperate about a new horse." I felt somebody had to be firm. "I think you should go to Corral Creek and look at the palomino anyway."

"If I have to have another horse," she said slowly, "I want a Mountain Lily."

Tom darted me an accusing look. For years I'd been telling Wezie stories about the Arabian stallion which, in early days, escaped his owner and ranged the Tobacco Root Mountains with a herd of wild horses. His diabolic cunning in escaping capture had earned him the name of Son of Satan. The stallion was long dead but his descendants, called Mountain Lilies, could sometimes be roped in the mountains.

For the most part they had degenerated into ugly, short-legged little beasts with over-large heads and stocky bodies. But even so, occasionally, when wild horses were rounded up to be shipped to the meat packers, a colt with something of Son of Satan's proud look turned up in the herd.

No rancher wanted a Lily running with his good stock, so Tom settled down to dissuade this child who could wrap him around her finger.

"I want a Mountain Lily," she told him again.

"You might have to wait a year to find a good one." But he was licked before Wezie said, "Then I'll wait."

There was no changing her mind. And somehow, as soon as the matter of the Mountain Lily was accepted by Tom and me a halcyon period descended on the ranch.

There was little wind that winter. The snow spread a glittering white carpet as far as the eye could see, its smooth surface marred only by tracks of wagons and trucks that hauled hay to the sheep camps and by the hooves of work and saddle horses. Sometimes when Wezie, Mrs. Buell and I braved the cold for an afternoon walk we found tiny lace-like tracks of birds quite close to the house. Then Wezie tied chunks of tallow in the willows along the creek so the feathered friends of Wigwam Canyon would not suffer.

The Chinook wind, one miracle of the north country that amazes me still, blew over the ranch in February. That night the snow began to melt and by morning water was running in all directions. Before we could believe it the ground was bare.

Jack got out the Montana State Nursery catalogue and pored over it. We consulted, made up a plant and seed order knowing all the while that our optimism was misplaced. But somehow the sight of bare ground always made spring seem closer.

It snowed again and again in March — in April. It was still bitter cold and the round-bellied stoves glowed red. Wezie and Mrs. Buell skied on the hills beyond the house, and skated on the beaver dams. The ranch hands got ready for lambing, repaired lanterns, mended tepees, cleaned out the sheds.

And then the trees and shrubs were a misty green. I saw a bluebird and knew it was spring.

"Mother! Mother!" Wezie called from the ditch bank one morning. "Look!" She pointed as I joined her.

Far down the canyon a flock of geese were headed our way. Closer and closer they came. We held our breath, afraid to speak, afraid we'd break the spell cast by that magic silver triangle that skimmed across the sky. We heard a wild, sweet honking. The geese were directly overhead when suddenly a lone bird broke the wedge, floated for a moment, wavered, dropped lower — lower.

"It's Sweet Adeline!" Wezie breathed softly. "She sees us, Mother." Her face was rapt, her blue eyes shining.

Then, just as suddenly as the lone goose had come, it wheeled and with a thrash of wings soared away to join the triangle.

I couldn't bear to look at Wezie now.

"I'm sorry — " I began, wanting to say it couldn't have been Adeline after all these years, that it was just another Canadian Honker looking for a place to nest; wanting to say something that would ease the hurt of my child's disappointment and not knowing how.

"Oh, no! Don't be sorry!" Wezie laughed and her laugh was a bubble of joy. "Adeline just stopped by to tell

us she's happy — that she loves us." She watched the geese
fade into the clouds that veiled the mountains, then dug
her hands deep into overall pockets in a way she had when
some problem was solved. "Adeline wanted us to know
she hasn't forgotten," she said.

Chapter Nine

JACK'S GARDEN, a quarter mile up the canyon, was the best in the valley. Our chore boy, at some time in his checkered career, had been under-gardener on an Irish estate; he knew everything there was to know about plants and soil. And he had a super-green thumb. He grew things that had no business putting out a leaf in the cold of Montana. Jack loved his plants as some people love children. I've seen him hover over a row of transplanted seedlings as though their very life depended upon his presence.

Our garden matured early. We were eating corn and ripe tomatoes two weeks before our neighbors. Jack's reputation spread far and wide and we let him bask in the fame but we knew — and he knew though he'd never admit it — that there were perfectly logical reasons for his extraordinary crops. For one thing his garden was sheltered from the wind on two sides by the walls of the canyon and on a third by a dense growth of chokecherry trees. Furthermore the water of Wigwam Creek, from which Jack irrigated, was warmer than most of the small streams in Montana.

Jack planted with a lavish hand. Tom couldn't get him to cut down on his garden. He'd agree but when harvest time came it was always the same. Year in and year out we gave surplus vegetables to anyone who would come and get them. And even after our root cellar was bulging with winter vegetables quantities still went to waste.

When I complained to Jack he inevitably came up with the same answer, "We'd ought to raise a few pigs." Jack liked pigs; his father had raised them in Ireland when he was a child. I didn't like pigs and neither did Tom but when he had a chance to take in a bred sow on a very old and very bad debt, he changed his way of thinking. Remembering Bitsie, and my flier in turkeys, I couldn't protest too much. Fortunately, I did inquire where he expected to keep the sow. He thought the far side of the chicken sheds would be the best place. "Easy to string up a fence there."

"Oh, no, you don't." The chicken sheds were too close to the house anyway. We'd talked for years of moving them down the creek but like most innovations on the Call Ranch this got no farther than talk. "I mean it, Tom. I don't intend to whiffle pig from now until fall."

Jack was loitering near the door. "I could throw up a fence at the Marsh place, Mum," he said. "You couldn't smell nothing from there."

The Marsh place, a short way up the creek, was one of the numerous homesteads that made up our ranch. It hadn't belonged to a Marsh in thirty years but it would go by that name until the end of time, as would the Arthur place, the Wright place, and a half dozen others.

Tom thought it over, then said the Marsh place was a mighty inconvenient distance to haul garbage. "And if I take this sow she's got to get along on vegetables and garbage," he warned because Jack had a bad habit of over-feeding any creature placed in his care.

"I could slop her easy when I go for the milch cows afternoons. 'Twouldn't be no trouble at all," Jack persisted.

Tom finally agreed, warning again, "Remember. Vegetables and garbage. Not one kernel of corn till the sow's pigs have to be fattened."

The sheep had always come first on our ranch and this year we scarcely had enough grain for lambing. We had reached a sorry pass if Tom could even consider depriving his ewes to fatten a bunch of not yet born shoats. I wanted to laugh reflecting how the mighty had fallen, ignominiously rooted out by a sow.

But Jack had got his way and lost no time preparing for his charge. He stretched a woven wire fence around part of an old corral at the Marsh place, built some feed and watering troughs and hauled in a load of straw. Shorty drove across the river for the sow that same week and brought her back to the ranch.

Before school, next morning, Wezie, Mrs. Buell and I walked up to the Marsh place with Tom to take a look at the hog. Jack, bucket in hand, was coming out of the pen. "Keep away from the fence, Wezie," he warned, then told me proudly, "she's a fine sow, Mum."

Maybe so, but the sow was the most grotesque beast I'd ever seen, and the filthiest. Mud plastered the rolls of fat that creased her flanks; mud completely covered her snoot and face. But mud couldn't hide the glint in her wicked eyes. And she smelled like nothing on this earth. Tom had to admit it.

"She's horrible." I held my nose, and started back to the house.

"Hey! Wait a minute." Tom was grinning. "How come you call her 'She'? You and Wezie have found a name for everything else on this ranch. Even some of the sheep."

I looked again at the gross, repulsive body, at the evil eyes, staring at me from beneath stiff white lashes.

"She was your idea. And Jack's," I said coldly. "So why don't one of you name her? Dainty Bess, or something equally fitting?"

"Dainty Bess!" Tom threw back his head and laughed his rare, infectious laugh that is like no other. "Dainty Bess! That suits me fine."

And so the beast came by her name.

I didn't see Dainty Bess again for two weeks but I knew she was with us on the occasions when the wind shifted and blew down creek. I complained to Tom, but Tom wasn't bothered about the smell any longer. He now had a more serious offense chalked up against Bess, or thought he had.

Hank, checking corn to make sure we had enough for lambing, discovered that four sacks were missing. The loss of corn is a serious matter; we can't grow it for feed because it seldom matures before heavy snowfall. Ours is shipped in from Kansas or Texas and can't be replaced overnight like wheat or oats which a neighbor would always be willing to sell or lend in an emergency.

Hank looked apoplectic when he told us of the theft. "Some moonshiner got those sacks!" Ordinarily the calmest and best mannered of men he forgot I was there and exploded into a profanity that was as colorful as it was strong. "'Scuse me, Mrs. Call," he apologized after a moment. "But it's me the herders'll blame if we run out of corn."

Tom reassured him, promised to look into the matter and report it to the Federal boys if he found any evidence at all, and Hank left for camp grumbling under his breath.

"You know darn well no moonshiner spirited that corn away," I said watching Hank climb into the buckboard. "Jack took it. He's up to his old trick of overfeeding. I'll bet you a mink pelt he's got those sacks cached around in the willows convenient to Bess."

"Of course. That's where the corn went," Tom agreed. "But don't let on to Hank. I won't have those two fellows feuding so close to lambing." He threw out his hands in a helpless gesture. "If I could just once catch that Irishman feeding corn — Never mind, just watch me get rid of that beast the minute her pigs are weaned. I'm looking forward with pleasure to the day I can trot her off to a butcher."

And from that day on he awaited the birth of Bess's brood with an anticipation I told him was predatory.

Eventually Bess brought seven piglets into the world, seven fat, corkscrew-tailed, spotted replicas of herself. (Years later, in his cups and embittered by Bess's ultimate betrayal of him, Jack weepingly admitted that there'd been an eighth pig, a cripple, which the sow devoured before he could come to its rescue.)

But Bess was a fond mother to the remaining seven. She guarded them with the fierce and unrelenting protectiveness of a she-bear. Only Jack was permitted near her pen. The moment anyone else approached she patrolled the fence, red-eyed and snorting fire.

Tom approached the fence fairly often. He dropped by Bess's pen at unlikely moments these days. The corn deal still rankled but he was too just a man to accuse Jack unless he had proof. One kernel of corn, overlooked by Bess, was all he needed and he was searching for it the morning he got too close to the fence and Bess snatched the knee out of his jeans.

He stared down at the gaping hole for a shocked second, gingerly felt his bare leg, then shook his fist at Bess who was busy disentangling a remnant of denim caught in her tusks. "Your days on this ranch are numbered, old girl!" he roared.

My heart stood still. I thought I must forbid Wezie to come near this pen and was about to caution Jack when I saw that his mild gray eyes were smouldering slits in a face as blank as a sheet of unused paper. There was a rigid set to his spine as he stalked past us.

"Now what's he sore about?" I wanted to know.

"You'd be surprised." Tom gave me a watered-down version of his genial smile. "Why the son-of-a-gun dotes on that vicious beast. It tickles his vanity because she's mean as hell with everybody but him. Proud of her too, even if she is a hog . . . told me she'd win a blue ribbon at the county fair if I'd let him have corn to condition her."

"I hope you nipped that scheme in the bud."

"You bet I did. But if I don't keep an eye on him, he'll snake it out right under my nose."

Fortunately, the season of the year was on Tom's side. We were caught up suddenly in the frantic melee of lambing. During the day herders and lambers were constantly fanning in and out of the granary, and Hank, still plenty sore about the missing corn, had warned the nightman to keep an eye on the rest of the grain. So Jack had no chance to smuggle extra rations to the sow.

But Bess, with an ingenuity you'd never expect to find in a hog, took care of the shortage. She broke through the sty fence and headed down creek to the garden, trailing her offspring along. Jack discovered them next morning and herded them back to the pen but not before they'd rooted up one end of the garden.

"A whole row of peas!" I groaned. This was indeed a disaster. Vegetables are scarce in Montana. The growing season is so short we're only sure of fresh garden truck about two months of the year.

" 'Twas my fault, Mum," Jack defended, gazing unhappily down a devastated row that had once been green peas. "I knew Bess'd been scratching herself on one of the fence posts. I'd ought to have checked to make sure it hadn't worked loose."

Tom was livid when told of the raid. "That settles it! Jack, you put those pigs on separated milk and slop. The day they're weaned we'll get rid of that sow."

And he checked on Jack frequently to be sure he

obeyed, to such good effect that two weeks later, the young pigs were guzzling separated milk and nosing into the slop. In another two weeks they were completely weaned and didn't need their mother any more. Tom got on the phone and finally sold Dainty Bess to a butcher in Twin Bridges.

"She's getting off this place Saturday morning," he announced with satisfaction.

"I bet old man Sorenson'd buy her for a brood sow and save you the trip," Jack ventured casually as if it was just a thought and didn't matter to him one way or another.

"I wouldn't sell that savage to my worst enemy, much less a neighbor," Tom replied flatly. "She's an outlaw, good for nothing but sausage."

I could see that Jack didn't take kindly to the idea of Bess converted into sausage, but he knew the Boss well enough to be sure it was useless to protest any more. He gloomed around for several days; then suddenly on Friday, the day before Bess was to leave us, he became his old cheerful self again. Apparently he was reconciled to the sow's departure, which rather surprised me. I'd never known him to give up so easily before.

But I understood why when Jack came in to breakfast on Saturday morning and informed us that Bess as well as her pigs had disappeared. "Gone without a trace," he announced with an air of innocence as spurious as the ring of a counterfeit silver dollar. "They was there at five — when I slopped 'em yesterday. But they're sure as anything gone now." He slid Tom a sidelong glance.

Tom's face was a study. He got madder and madder as

breakfast progressed. I wanted to laugh at the neat way Jack had outwitted us. And if I knew our choreboy there wouldn't be so much as a hoofprint to show where Bess had gone. I choked on a giggle and Tom glared at me. He didn't mean to let Jack get away with this. Breakfast half-eaten, he shoved back his chair, grabbed a hat and strode through the door. Jack and I followed, hard put to keep up.

The pen seemed tight. Tom checked the fence posts one by one, kicking each with the toe of his boot. They were tight too.

"That sow didn't sprout wings. And she wouldn't have left of her own accord —" He fixed Jack with a hard, stern look, "I want to know how she got out of this pen."

"Somebody must of stole her and trucked her away."

"O.K. Just show me a truck track."

"Somebody could have shot her and caught the shoats." Jack's eyes were artless, his voice without guile.

"That won't do, Buckley. Where did you take the sow and her pigs?"

Now, Jack knew he was on touchy ground when Tom called a man by his last name and he looked a little shaken, but he still denied any part in the pigs' abduction.

"What would I be doing with them?" he inquired, but not, I thought, with the righteous indignation of an innocent man accused. He would not back down although Tom hammered away at him for a good half hour. Furthermore he insisted upon joining Tom and Hank when they set out to look for the pigs. They flushed the willows on either side of the creek for a mile and finally gave up without finding a single trace of Bess or her family.

"That Irishman knows where they are!" Tom railed when, sweaty, scratched, and weary, he got back to the house. "He could have staked them out in any one of a hundred gullies and he's safe because he knows I haven't got time to hunt them down. I just can't figure it out . . . Why he'd go to all that trouble — sneaking them away after dark, wiping out every last track. How did he do it? He couldn't have carried Bess; she must weigh a half ton . . . I've got it!" He clapped both hands on his knees. "I'll bet he lured her off with a bucket of corn. And I bet I saw the very bucket upended on the fence."

"How are you going to prove it?"

"I can't. I can't even figure why he'd do such a thing."

I could. Behind that guise of stolid indifference, Jack was as tenderhearted as a child. He was the sworn defender of every helpless, put-upon creature, big or small. In Bess's case it was simple. He had a real affection for the sow and her family and couldn't bear to see them end up on a butcher's block. But Jack's compassion went deeper than that. I had seen him rescue and turn a mouse loose in a grain box because a cat was tormenting it. And that when the barn was overrun with mice and we were doing everything we could to get rid of them.

Jack didn't know I had seen him. I slipped quietly away, oddly touched by the look of pity on that rough, weathered face. I didn't tell Tom. I wasn't quite sure at the time that a man raised in this hard country would understand . . .

It was August before we heard of Bess again. Hank

sighted her while moving a sheep camp. "It was old Bess, all right," he reported. "I'd know her anywhere. But she's wilder'n a coyote now and so's her shoats."

Tom looked troubled. "I don't like it," he fretted. "Lord help us if a bunch of wild hogs overrun this ranch. They'll even go after lambs if they get hungry enough. Eat meat and pelt and bone. I've seen it happen. It's that Irishman's fault," he exploded angrily. "I've a notion to tell him to roll his bed and get down the road."

I was far more concerned over the idea of Jack's departure than the remote possibility of hogs killing lambs. Jack was my second pair of hands. There was no task too hard or too humble for him. Besides milking, churning, tending garden, chopping and hauling wood to the six heaters in our house, Jack separated the milk, washed the separator and took care of the chickens. I couldn't have raised my children without him. He'd rescued them when they might have drowned in the creek, hauled them out from mean horses' hooves, doctored their cuts and bruises and wasn't even above baby-sitting on occasions. Jack was indispensable if anyone could be indispensable on a ranch. I said so. But Tom was just letting off steam. He wouldn't fire Jack.

"Damn it! He knows I won't fire him," Tom conceded. "But if he'd just admit he turned those pigs loose I'd feel better about it."

This Jack never admitted. And he went around all that summer in the best possible spirits never dreaming that his act of mercy would boomerang and strike him where it hurt the most. For Bess, with no gratitude whatever for past favors, suddenly swooped down on the ranch again that autumn, this time sabotaging poor old Jack's annual vacation.

Every fall after the winter vegetables were stowed away in the root cellar my second pair of hands drew his "time" — a full year's wages — and went on a terrific binge. Since this was his only form of entertainment and he did the work of two men the rest of the year nobody begrudged him a vacation, least of all Tom and I.

But Jack never approached anything in a straight line. All of his maneuvers were circuitous. He couldn't even go on a spree for the "hell-of-it" like an ordinary ranch hand. He had to work himself up, nip by nip, until he reached such a diabolical state of belligerency that Tom was compelled to take him to town to keep peace on the ranch. To Jack's way of thinking, this put the blame for his defection squarely on Tom.

There was only one hitch to Jack's plan. He had to have liquor for the nips that would gradually transform him from a kind, considerate person into what the rest of the men called a "devil-on-wheels." No ranch hand was willing to give him that first drink because if he did, he would be expected to take over Jack's chores as well as his own. A powerful deterrent. Hence, if Jack worked himself into a proper state of temper he had to make his own liquor, a potent brew which he concocted from chokecherries.

The finest chokecherries were those that sheltered the garden. Each year when the fruit reached a certain state of ripeness, Jack gathered the clusters (secretly, he thought, but we all knew and respected his secret), packed them in heavy paper cartons and hid them in the willows.

Now, September was wet and cold the fall that Bess betrayed the only friend she had. Jack was late getting the winter vegetables in; but his chokecherries had been picked for days, hidden in the willows, ready to be put down in stone crocks when he found time and privacy to do it.

Dainty Bess, on the other hand, had plenty of time and, enjoying the privacy of a big ranch, beat him to it. She and her brood of wild hogs found the chokecherries, over-turned the boxes, ate their fill and trampled what was left into the ground. The timing was unfortunate for at this late season no more chokecherries were to be found.

Jack didn't go to town that year and we didn't know why until Hank, searching for an old ewe, ran on to the evidence. "It sure was a mess," he told us grinning broadly. "Must of been the whole bunch of hogs stomping round, the way the bushes was broke. They even smashed those big stone crocks Jack uses to age the stuff in."

That winter was one of little snow and bitter winds and cold. April and May were no better. Again we went into a summer of drought. The springs and small creeks were a mere trickle of their former volume, and every drop of water was precious. Consequently Jack, frightened like the rest of us, planted only a fourth of his usual vegetable garden. Things looked bleak at the Call Ranch.

Apparently things looked even bleaker for Bess and her wild brood for they deserted the foothills and ranged closer to the home place. One morning we awakened to find half our vegetable garden uprooted. Cloven hoof tracks were thick all through the devastated furrows. Seething, Tom replaced a broken fence post. He strung an extra wire close to the ground. A few mornings later there were signs of an attempted raid but no break through.

"I'd like to of seen her face when she rooted into that bobwire," Jack exclaimed spitefully and I knew by the tone of his voice how Bess's treachery had eaten into his soul.

"The minute we get through haying, I'm going to give every man on this ranch a gun and a horse and we're going to have a hog hunt to end all hog hunts," Tom said.

True to his word, the day after haying was over the men set out at daybreak. They returned after dark, discouraged and hungry, with the report that they'd got all seven young hogs, but Bess the intrepid was still at large. Tom, Jack and Hank hunted again. Nobody left the ranch without a gun, but nobody sighted Bess. We never knew whether she was wounded on the first hunt and went into the hills to die — where a coyote later devoured her — or whether she was smart enough to change her theatre of operation. At any rate, we never saw or heard of her again.

But I noticed, in chokecherry season, that Jack's head was apt to lift at any unusual sound or scent from up the canyon. Alive or dead, Dainty Bess's corpulent ghost continued to haunt the Call Ranch for many a year to come.

Chapter Ten

IT WAS WEZIE, after all, who found the Mountain Lily —
or rather chance and her tender, compassionate heart sin-
gled him out. More than a year had passed since we made
our pact with her. Twice Tom had got on the trail of a
Mountain Lily and each time been disappointed. The first
horse was much too old, the second did not have a good
conformation. And now lambing was at hand and he
wouldn't have time to look any more.

January, February and most of March Patches had been
running with a string of unbroken horses we kept pastured
in the mountains. He preferred them to the work and
saddle horses that were pastured nearer home. There was
no question of Wezie riding the pony when winter gave
way to spring. She'd grown unbelievably in the past year;
was almost as tall as I. And every inch of growth had been
sorrow to her. She hated growing up with a passion.

When I suggested we buy a new bed to replace the
youth's bed in her room she said, "I don't want a new bed.
I like to sleep doubled up." The only clothes that interested her were western clothes, levis, shirts, and boots.

It was a battle to get her into a shop for anything else.

And she clung to Patches. Even though she'd quit riding him she spent hours with the little horse, leading him out on the flat to graze, currying his spotted coat until it shone, combing his mane and tail, even plaiting them.

Patches loved all this attention. I doubt if he cared whether she rode him or not; just to be with her, to have her undivided love was enough. Patches didn't know that this period of happy content would soon be over; that a Mountain Lily would soon share Wezie's devotion.

Hank saw the Lily first. He came home one day at noon nursing a black eye and told us he'd had a run-in with a herder of Bill Anderson's.

"Caught him working a horse over; whacking it on the head with a club." Hank rubbed skinned knuckles and smiled with grim satisfaction. "I gave the skunk a dose of his own medicine. He won't be beating another horse soon."

"I hope you stopped by and told Bill about it?" Tom was in town but I knew he'd want our neighbor to have the straight facts of the story. Hank had broken an unwritten law. He should have immediately reported the abuse of the horse to Bill instead of taking matters into his own hands. Herders are a close-knit lot, jealous of any outside interference. A thing like this could cause bad blood between the men on our two ranches.

"I thought you could phone him," Hank said. "I've got another camp to tend."

"Oh, Hank, I wish you'd gone straight to Bill. I wish you'd stayed out of this —"

"Mother! How could he? That awful herder was beating a horse!" Wezie's eyes were blazing; she was angrier than I'd ever seen her, but she found time to get a slab of raw beef for Hank's eye and iodine for his knuckles. And all the time she was plying him with questions. Had he brought the club away so the herder couldn't use it again? Yes, he had. Was the horse badly hurt? Bloodied around the head, Hank said, then noting her distress hastened to add, "He'll be as good as new in a couple of weeks so quit your worrying. You can't down a Lily. They're tough."

"A Lily?"

"Yep. The one Bill found bogged down in a snow bank last winter."

"So that's the horse," Wezie said slowly.

She would have gone to Bill's anyway, Lily or no. Nothing could have kept her from checking on that horse's injuries. The minute school was over she persuaded Jack to drive her to our neighbor's in the buckboard. When she got back Tom was home and she rushed through the house to his office leaving a trail of snow and ice behind her.

"I've found my Lily, Daddy! You'll never guess —" She was so excited, she talked so fast he had to slow her down to understand. When she finished he said, "I'll have to check a little, Wezie. If the horse is injured, I can't let you have him."

"He's not injured, Daddy . . . I mean he is, but he'll heal. I'll doctor him." The look that had brought many an animal back from the jaws of death settled down on her face. "I want him, Daddy."

"How do you know Bill wants to sell him?"

"He doesn't. But I persuaded him. He said he would if it was all right with you. I told him it was."

Here we go again, I thought. She wants this horse because he's been hurt, because she thinks he needs her. Another waif to be cared for, worried over — "What does he look like?" I asked, resigned.

"He's shiny black, with a star on his forehead. I've decided to call him Son-of-Satan after his grandfather." She took it for granted the horse would be hers, and sighed happily. "He's beautiful, Mother. I can't wait for you to see him. Oh, Daddy, couldn't I bring him home tomorrow?"

"No," Tom said firmly. He didn't want her to become attached to a horse whose injuries might well be permanent. But he'd better have given in for she went over to the Anderson Ranch every chance she got and she telephoned to inquire about the horse the days she couldn't go. I'm sure that Bill was glad to be rid of the Lily when Tom finally agreed to bring him home. That day, he and Wezie set out in the pick-up right after school.

As the truck rattled past the house I saw her saddle and bridle in back and ran toward the gate shouting to stop them.

"Surely you're not going to let that child ride a strange horse home alone?" I couldn't believe Tom would let her do it. As a rule he was far more cautious than I.

Wezie giggled and Tom looked sheepish. "She's been riding him bareback for over a week," he told me. And he'd been watching her. In the middle of lambing, he'd found time to turn up at the Anderson Ranch when he knew she was there. He grinned, "You're too nosy. She wanted to surprise you."

And to give me less time to interfere, I thought. They weren't fooling me. Wezie was an excellent rider but she was just a little girl and Mountain Lilies were often unpredictable. I'd have wanted her to work this one out first in our own corral. And they knew it.

I was restless and uneasy, and made a number of trips to the window before I heard the pound of hoofbeats coming down the hill. Still another trip to the window — and this time I saw a flash of blue overall, flying blonde hair and the radiant face of my child as she galloped past on the Mountain Lily.

Patches, munching grass along the creek, saw his little friend too. He jerked up his head, flattened his ears, backed up a few steps and let out a shrill, outraged whinny. Poor Patches, I knew how he felt as well as if I'd been a horse myself.

The Mountain Lily wasn't as beautiful as Wezie thought him but he wasn't bad looking if you took him all in one piece. His coat was satin black and he had a good head. He had the look of a spirited horse but actually he was gentle and trustworthy and certainly did not live up to his name Son-of-Satan. (Which was just as well because that name only survived until the ranch men discovered that Bill had called him Nig. Then Nig it became.)

Patches whinnied again and this time flung his head from side to side. Anybody could have read the little fellow's mind. Here in the flesh was the fiery steed that Patches fancied himself. Worse still it was apparent that the usurper was fast worming his way into Wezie's affection, something not to be tolerated. Patches picked up his hoofs and raced toward the barn bent on mischief. But Wezie had the black horse inside the corral and the gate shut before he reached it.

Her eyes were bright with unshed tears when she came to the house. "I did it all wrong," she mourned. "I should have put Patches in the barn so he couldn't see me on another horse. Now I've hurt his feelings."

Ever since she had first agreed to a Mountain Lily Wezie had planned how to ride him with the least hurt to Patches.

"I'll do it a little bit at a time, Mother. And Patches can follow us everywhere we go. Just like Missie," she told me softly. "Oh, Mother, remember how Missie loved to follow us?"

But Patches was a different kettle of fish. He didn't like any part of it. The first time he followed, Wezie came home in a state.

"Patches nipped at Nig all the way and kicked him every time he got the chance," she told us. "I don't know what I'm going to do."

Tom knew what he was going to do. "We'll have no more of that," he informed her sternly. "One of these days he'll try one of his tricks on a narrow trail and the black horse will bolt and spill you down the mountain. Patches can't follow any more."

"He won't stay at home," Wezie wailed. "And besides, think how it would hurt his feelings if we shut him in the corral."

"Well, his feelings are due to be hurt," Tom said flatly. "He's not going to follow Nig any more."

"But Daddy, he's never been shut up. He's always waiting for me at the gate in the morning. He won't understand. He'll think nobody's friends with him anymore and you just don't know how he'll grieve."

"He'll just have to grieve." Tom could be firm where Wezie's welfare was concerned. But even Tom was surprised at the violence of Patches' grief. The first time Wezie rode off without him the little horse went completely berserk. He tore around the corral like a wild thing, bucking back and front, snorting his protests, trying to jump the high pole fence. I rode with Wezie that Saturday morning and we could hear his outraged protests until we were more than a mile away from the ranch.

Wezie was heartbroken; I couldn't get her to talk. After a time I saw she was crying.

"Don't take it so hard, honey." I rode close and squeezed her arm. "Why, you're as bad as Patches. But Patches will get over it. You'll see."

"No, he won't," her breath caught on a sob. "He thinks I like Nig the best. Oh Mother, how can I show him I love him more than I ever did?"

"You'll think of something," I comforted. "Just put your mind to it." And she did.

The moment we got home, she unsaddled Nig, shut him in the barn, went to the corral and led the little horse out. I can see them yet, side by side, trudging up the hill beyond the bunkhouse. They were gone a long time and when she got back she told me they'd walked almost to Dry Hollow. "Patches loved it, and Mother I've promised myself that every time I ride Nig I'll come home and take Patches out."

It was obvious that this extra attention assuaged Patches' grief and frustration not one whit. He kicked and squealed and tried to jump the corral fence every time he saw Wezie lead Nig from the barn. He lamed himself lashing out at the gate.

Wezie was frantic. She couldn't study; her grades fell off —

"You'll have to do something about that pony," Mrs. Buell told Tom. "Wezie can't keep her mind on anything else."

The problem was eventually solved by Jack. "We'll fool the little divil," he told Wezie. "I'll saddle Nig and bring him to the back of the house. Then you can ride down Canyon and Patches won't even see you." So with Jack's connivance the situation improved for a time. But Wezie still kept the promise she'd made herself. No matter how tired she was, she always took the pony for an outing when she returned from a ride on Nig.

Patches wasn't mollified. He nursed his grievance and never lost a chance to nip or lash out with his hoofs when he got close to the black horse. And it was a nuisance to keep them apart.

Patches had the run of the place and the men were in and out of the barn, frequently leaving the door open. When Nig got loose there was always trouble. Eventually the Lily, who hadn't deigned to notice this persecution before, began to retaliate. Nearly always the smaller, fleeter horse had the advantage in a running battle. But Nig possessed heavier hoofs and stronger teeth and he used them to good advantage. So more and more that summer

Patches returned to the hills to run with the unbroken string. The only time Tom tried to bring him back, he escaped and returned the same day.

At first Wezie felt betrayed and bitterly hurt by his defection. Then, surprisingly, she accepted it with a cheerfulness that baffled and shocked me.

"Wouldn't you like to have Hank bring Patches down?" I asked her several times. She always said no.

One day when I knew Tom would be riding fence near the horse pasture I suggested that he bring Patches down. "I feel sorry for that little fellow, Wezie."

"Mother, you don't understand," she told me gravely. "Patches likes to be free. But he likes to *belong* too; and now that nobody rides him he's happier up there with his friends. He likes those horses and he likes —" The words trailed away but there was a little, tucked-in smile on her lips.

This didn't make sense either. I searched her face anxiously.

"Don't look so solemn and worried, Mother!" She laughed now — a gay, bubbling laugh that was so infectious I had to laugh too. "Be happy for Patches. I think he's found Missie." She flung both arms about my neck and hugged me. "Oh, Mother I *know* he's found Missie. He's just bound to have found her or he'd never stay up there in the mountains so long."

She always believed it and, happy for Patches, was willing to let the little horse go.

She grew closer to Nig as the summer progressed but the relationship was never the same as with Patches. Patches had been like another child, a loved companion, someone to share everything. She was fond of Nig and proud of him but I noticed she never went out to give him a good-night pat or a kiss, as she had with Patches.

Yet she was fiercely possessive of the black horse and would never let anyone else ride him, not even her brothers or Tom.

"Don't you think you're a little selfish?" I asked one day when she'd refused to let a stranded herder ride Nig the five miles to his sheep camp.

"No, I don't, Mother," she told me solemnly. "What would you say if someone wanted to borrow me or one of the boys? Besides, Nig has his feelings too." She stroked Nig's glossy mane and he whinnied softly. "You're just like Patches, Mother. You don't understand."

I felt a sudden kinship for the little pony. Wezie loved us both but she'd outgrown Patches and she'd taken the first long step away from me toward an adult world. She was still a child but she was well able to do her own thinking, and to her Nig deserved the same consideration and respect that she gave her family.

And so the black horse took Patches' place in Wezie's life but never in her heart.

Chapter Eleven

WINTER CAME EARLY. A glaze iced over the snow so that the sheep wouldn't paw through to grass and had to be fed from Thanksgiving on. The drifts and constant blizzards made it impossible to haul hay to the camps and for the first time I saw the flock, all six bands of them, herded to the home ranch.

The sheep bleated day and night, their mournful "baas" mingling with the wind that howled against the eaves of the house and hurled the snow in all directions. A wicked winter. A question in every woolgrower's eyes. Would the hay hold out until spring? Would the sheep survive? Nobody could tell, but the Calls had something far worse to worry about.

One night, early in January, Wezie became violently ill. Friends brought their shovels and cleared the road as quickly as possible but even so it was hours before we could take her to a Butte hospital. There we learned that she had a rare virus infection, which baffled the doctors. There was nothing they could do.

Tom and I sat by her bed around the clock, but not all

our love nor all our prayers could save her. Wezie died three days later.

Tom was the strong one then. I don't know how I could have lived through that stretch of time without him.

"This is the worst," he whispered at the cemetery. "Nothing can ever again be so bad."

But Tom was wrong. The worst was going home. We didn't talk on the way back . . . I'd been staring ahead, blindly — dreading the first sight of the ranch, when Tom exclaimed, "For God's sake, look!" and stopped the car.

We'd reached the gate and there, on the other side, heads close together, stood Wezie's two horses Patches and Nig. Patches had been high in the mountains with the unbroken horses, Nig with the work and saddle horses in a pasture nearer the ranch. Fifteen miles apart. Yet some amazing instinct had brought them together; these two that could never meet without lashing and biting and furious neighing, were standing quietly side by side.

Tom put his hand over mine. "They're not fighting any more," he said in an odd hoarse voice.

Of course not. They know they haven't anything to fight over now. Wezie's dead. But I said this in my heart and kept it inside because I could see that the sudden cessation of hostilities between the two horses meant something to Tom, in some way comforted him.

I kept a number of things to myself that winter. I kept to myself that the house which had once been a home was now just four walls and a roof; that every blank, empty day that I walked through was exactly the same as another — only longer.

"Would you like to have the boys come home?" Tom asked me one night. "Would that help?" His anxiety made me ashamed. I'd been nursing my own grief, not thinking of him. And I'd been pushing Wezie out of my mind with every conscious thought. Now I tried to bring her back and couldn't . . . I couldn't see my little girl who had rushed through life like a mountain stream . . .

The rest of that winter passed slowly. Finally the snow abated. The hay held out. The sheep were driven back to their camps and the tracks of the hay wagons were seen again on the snow-covered hills. Preparations for lambing began . . . The quaking aspen misted with green . . . One day I saw a bluebird . . . Again it was spring, but there was no spring in my heart.

Jack got out the seed catalogue, we consulted and I mailed an order to the State Nursery and wondered painfully if the time would ever come when I could take an interest in the ranch again. The answer came in a strange and wonderful way . . .

I was walking up the path to the garden early one morning when I heard a distant familiar sound. In spite of the pang it brought to my heart I turned and searched the sky. Far down the canyon a silver skein of geese were moving toward me. I didn't want to watch but something held me; I couldn't move.

The birds were coming closer. Their wild, sweet honks were now as clear as a bell. They were overhead . . . Suddenly a lone goose broke away from the triangle, as on a morning I remembered too well. The great gray bird floated with effortless grace for a moment, then dropped lower and lower — circled the ranch buildings slowly and with a powerful thrash of wings soared upward to disappear over the mountains in the wake of the flock.

I closed my eyes . . . saw a rapt young face . . . heard a vibrant voice that was filled with gladness.

Oh, No! Don't be sorry. Adeline just stopped by to tell us she's happy . . . that she loves us . . . That she hasn't forgotten.

I stood for a long moment . . . And there on the garden path in the gentle light of a new day I found the strength to open the door of her little kingdom and let my child go. I felt a rush of almost forgotten warmth, as if Wezie had touched my hand. Then suddenly, wondrously, I knew that she was still a part of our lives and the ranch she loved — the canyon, the creek, the mountains, the rushing winds, the very air that we breathed.